WHAT ARE THEY SAYING ABOUT
THEOLOGICAL REFLECTION?

What Are They Saying About Theological Reflection?

Robert L. Kinast

PAULIST PRESS
New York/Mahwah, N.J.

Cover design by James Brisson

Copyright © 2000 by Robert L. Kinast

Library of Congress Cataloging-in-Publication Data

Kinast, Robert L.
    What are they saying about theological reflection? / Robert L. Kinast.
       p.   cm.—(WATSA series)
    Includes bibliographical references.
    ISBN 0-8091-3968-5 (alk. paper)
    1. Theology—Methodology. I. Title. II. Series.

BR118 .K6174 2000
230'.01—dc21

                                          00-038513

Published by Paulist Press
997 Macarthur Boulevard
Mahwah, New Jersey 07430

www.paulistpress.com

Printed and bound in the
United States of America

Contents

To my friends and colleagues
who have supported the Center for Theological Reflection

To Jim and Evelyn, Tom, Patricia and John, Rebecca and Beth,
Bob and Don
for their timely and helpful feedback

and
To Judith
who sustains me in all things

1
Introduction

Theological reflection has become the term for a distinct form of theologizing that has emerged over the last twenty-five years. Yet the term itself does not reveal very much about this form of theologizing. The word theo-*logy* implies some type of reflective activity, while the object of theological reflection—God—is an all-encompassing topic.

The distinctiveness of this form of theologizing is better suggested by other terms that are sometimes used—*contextual theology, experiential theology, praxis theology.* Theological reflection works out of specific contexts rather than working with generic truths. It draws upon lived experience as much as classic texts. It aims at practical action, not theoretical ideas. Its distinctiveness is further conveyed by the several sources that have contributed to its development—Latin American liberation theology, feminist theology, Black and Hispanic/Latino theology, catechetical theology, clinical pastoral education, spiritual renewal and ecumenical dialogue.[1]

What all these sources and synonyms have in common is a deceptively simple threefold movement. It begins with the lived experience of those doing the reflection; it correlates this experience with the sources of the Christian tradition; and it draws out practical implications for Christian living. On the surface this is a natural, commonsense way of functioning. It reflects the way most

1

people think practically. But beneath the surface there are many complexities that are best expressed as questions.

    Experience: What type of experience is suitable for theological reflection; who decides; how is the chosen experience extracted from the context in which it occurs and is shared with others; in a group or community setting whose experience is given priority; is every experience already theological or is it made theological by being correlated with the sources of faith?

    Faith tradition: Which sources are used for correlation with a particular experience; who decides; how are those sources interpreted and who determines the accuracy and validity of the interpretation; how are conflicting sources or interpretations handled; what role does the chosen experience play in interpreting the faith tradition; how much theology does a person need to know before doing theological reflection; is theological reflection a way of gaining theological knowledge; how are discrete reflections combined into a systematic or comprehensive whole?

    Practical implications for Christian living: How does a person move from the level of reflection to the level of behavior; who decides whether a suggested praxis is consistent with Christian belief; how is this determined; how does a person insure that praxis flows from reflection; how is a given praxis implemented and evaluated; what is needed to keep the process ongoing?

    By itself the common form of theological reflection does not answer these questions. It is neither a method (in the sense that apologetic, scholastic, transcendental, historical-critical forms of theology are methods), nor is it a separate theological discipline (in the sense that biblical, historical, systematic, moral and pastoral theology are distinct disciplines). Theological reflection is a form of theology in the sense that David Tracy discusses it.[2] Noting that, for the ancients, "the essence of the real and our knowledge of it consists ultimately of form," Tracy appeals for a recovery of this central principle so that education might once again become formation in the symbols, narratives, rituals, doctrines and theories of tradition. Of course, the existing forms of a tradition do not preclude the emergence of new forms. In fact a living tradition is characterized by its ability to generate new forms through which the reality of that tradition may come through more richly and fully.[3]

This is what theological reflection seeks to do—to allow the reality of theology to come through its distinct form, namely, experience correlated with tradition for the sake of praxis. The reality of theology, which theological reflection seeks to disclose, is the presence of God in people's experience, a presence that invites them to encounter God where they are and to participate in the divine life which is offered to them there. For this reason the form that theological reflection takes is coextensive with people's experience. It does not treat their experience as a theological or spiritual void nor does it use their experience merely to illustrate and apply theological principles. With theological reflection, theology is in service to experience, not the other way around.

Styles of Theological Reflection

How exactly does the common form of theological reflection work in practice? To answer that question, and the other questions listed above, it is necessary to look to the various styles of theological reflection that the common form has generated. Five of these styles will be examined in the following chapters. They are ministerial, spiritual wisdom, feminist, inculturation and practical. In each case, except the feminist style, one or two primary representatives will be the focus of attention. For reasons explained in chapter 3, a feminist style of theological reflection does not lend itself to the same type of presentation.

Describing each of these examples as a style of theological reflection maintains the aesthetic quality implied by the notion of form, but it also carries some risk. In ecclesiastical culture, and to some degree in popular culture, style is not valued very highly.[4]

Usually it is contrasted with substance and treated as a peripheral and possibly deceptive way of expressing the substance of a person (with the further implication that substance alone is what counts). A closer look reveals that style should not be so easily dismissed.

First of all, the interplay of substance and style is a variation on the relationship between form and content. The two always go together, and to split them is one of the three fatal separations of modern Western culture, according to David Tracy (the other two being the split between feeling-thought and theory-practice).[5] Although great strides have been made in recent decades to heal the rupture between feeling-thought and theory-practice, the separation of form and content (or style and substance) has hardly been recognized, much less overcome. In part this is because thought does not always pay enough attention to experience. In reality everyone functions with a certain style.

Parents may exhibit a loving or domineering style with their children; teachers may use a transmissive or collaborative style with students; athletes may develop an attention-getting or team-oriented style of play; leaders may give orders (authoritarian style) or strive for consensus (relational style). Authors develop a writing style, business executives a management style, lecturers a speaking style, entertainers a performing style and virtually everyone a lifestyle.

The style a person adopts indicates what that person values and prefers, how the person responds to other people and situations, what the person's feelings and tendencies are, and ultimately who the person is. Regarding theology, a confessional or evangelical style proclaims theological truth for others to accept, whereas an apologetic style argues for the cogency of theological beliefs so others may be convinced. A devotional style accents the affective dimension of theology, while a scholastic style emphasizes the cognitive. A dogmatic style suggests authoritative definition, whereas a liberal style suggests a toleration of all viewpoints, and an ecumenical style implies openness to diverse opinions with a view toward consensus.

Similarly a theological reflection style is determined by the type of experience practitioners of that style focus on, how they correlate it with the faith tradition and what sort of praxis they envision emerging from their reflection. These three points will be the basis for presenting and comparing the five styles of theological reflection to follow.

The styles themselves correspond to a gradually widening range of experience and breadth of praxis. A ministerial style is the most limited, focusing on experiences and praxis within the context of church ministry. A spiritual wisdom style goes beyond this, being open to the full range of life experience but with a view toward Christian formation and the appropriation of the faith tradition. A feminist style goes further still by critiquing and reconstructing the faith tradition. It does this from the perspective of women's experience, not just in the church but also in society, not just in the present but also historically. Likewise the praxis it envisions is a transformation of both church and society toward a more holistic, integral relationship between women and men.

An inculturation style embraces the experience of both men and women as it is shaped by and contributes to the local and global culture. It shares the same critical and constructive impulse of a feminist style and directs this impulse toward new cultural expressions of the gospel. Finally a practical style examines the experience of both religious and secular communities as they engage society in all its aspects. The underlying aim is to reveal the theological implications of current praxis and to strategize for more effective praxis going forward.

Not all of these styles use the term *theological reflection* to describe their work but all of them share the common form of theological reflection. Their similarities and differences indicate the richness of theological reflection at the present time and what theologians are saying about it.

2
A Ministerial Style of Theological Reflection

The term *theological reflection* is probably best known and most widely used in the training of men and women for church ministry, especially in the supervisory and field-education components of their training. Undoubtedly the best-known and most widely used text for theological reflection in this setting is *Method in Ministry* by James and Evelyn Eaton Whitehead.[1] Originally published in 1980 and revised in 1995, it is the standard for a ministerial style of theological reflection.

The Whiteheads' *Method in Ministry*

The Whiteheads understand theological reflection to be "the process of bringing to bear in the practical decisions of ministry the resources of Christian faith."[2] In this sense theological reflection is not new. However, the contemporary ministerial context in which it takes place is new because it is more complex than ever. The human sciences constantly reveal how complex human situations and relationships are; critical methods in theology show how complex and diverse the faith tradition is; behavioral science and systems analysis indicate how difficult it is to translate ideas into practice. This situation calls for a method of reflection to help

Christians understand the gospel more clearly and carry it out more effectively. Such a method will be characterized in three ways: it must be portable so Christians can carry it into their daily lives, performable so they can translate their reflections into action and communal so they can face today's challenges together.

In responding to these demands, the Whiteheads present a model within a method.[3] The *model* consists of three sources of information relevant to ministerial decision making and practice: the faith tradition, personal and communal experience and contemporary culture. Their style of theological reflection entails a conversation among these three sources.[4]

In explicating this model, the Whiteheads begin with the faith tradition. This is somewhat surprising given the usual emphasis (endorsed by the Whiteheads) of beginning theological reflection with lived experience. But starting with tradition helps to clarify two important points: The use of personal and communal experience for theological reflection is always set within the context of faith, and such experience is not the primary, and certainly not the only, norm of religious truth.

For the Whiteheads the faith tradition embraces all the sources of the Christian heritage, with scripture holding pride of place. These sources are not timeless and absolute bits of information; they are the testimony concerning the ways human beings have experienced God in history. As a result, the faith tradition exhibits a great diversity of expressions and practices at its origin, throughout its history and in its human-divine constitution. On the one hand this can be bewildering and confusing; on the other hand it can be liberating and enriching. The difference depends on whether theological reflection can help people befriend the pluriformity of their faith tradition.

The Whiteheads' emphasis on both personal and communal experience offsets a cultural tendency toward individualism (and in the realm of ministerial training, toward clericalism). It also directs theological reflection to an important but often neglected authority—the sense of the faithful. This is where tradition and experience have met in the past and where they overlap today. An appreciation for the role that the sense of the faithful has played in history encourages contemporary communities of faith to engage their tradition actively rather than submissively as they respond to current challenges.

The inclusion of the resources of culture is one of the distinctive contributions that the Whiteheads have made to the general form of theological reflection. Like the faith tradition, cultural life is complex and ambiguous, sometimes challenging the faith tradition, sometimes contributing to it and sometimes contradicting it. This is not perceived as a threat or a problem to be overcome but as one of the conditions for carrying out honest, realistic theological reflection.

Three-Stage Method

The Whiteheads' *method* of theological reflection moves through three stages. The first calls for reflectors to attend (listen) to the information yielded by the three sources of the model. The second stage expects a lively conversation among these sources with reflectors asserting their personal convictions while being open to other points of view. Unless this conversation is short-circuited by either a domineering aggressiveness or a passive nonassertiveness, a consensus or shared understanding should emerge (which the Whiteheads liken to a crucible where diverse materials are transformed into a single substance). This leads to the third stage—an appropriate pastoral response. This stage typically includes planning, implementing and evaluating in order to put the reflectors' decision into practice.

These stages correspond to the general three-step form of theological reflection (which the Whiteheads helped to solidify). They elaborate each step with theoretical perspectives, drawn mostly from the social sciences, and practical recommendations, drawn from pastoral cases. The former manifests theological reflection's interdisciplinary openness and helps to ground personal reflection in a more scientific body of information. The latter helps to keep this style of theological reflection rooted in its primary goal of aiding the practice of ministry.

The attending stage of the method is a demanding exercise because it takes into account far more than personal feelings and desires, preferences and preconceptions. It requires persistent openness and ministerial asceticism to listen actively for the truth, however it may appear, and to respond with accurate understanding, evidenced by empathy and the ability to paraphrase another's point of view.[5]

Equally demanding is the second stage because reflectors are expected to allow all the relevant sources from the model to interact in a relatively unbiased conversation. Asserting one's theological convictions does not mean simply declaring "what I believe." It means making an informed judgment based on an awareness of today's religious pluralism and an acceptance of the adult responsibility to claim and hand on the faith effectively. Both stages require intellectual and spiritual maturity as well as a confidence that truth and meaning will emerge through the conversation rather than being brought ready-made to the discussion and imposed upon the experience. This degree of maturity cannot simply be presumed, which is one reason why the Whiteheads recommend that theological reflection take place in a group that is well facilitated.

The theological reflection process is not complete until the reflectors have decided on the most appropriate course of action that their reflection suggests and have planned the steps to implement it. Practical action based on theological principles has always been an ideal of Christian ministry, but too often in the past theological principles were worked out in isolation from the practical situations in which they were to be applied. This left pastoral practitioners to rely on their own rules of thumb or on an anecdotal sense of "what works" in applying theology to ministry.[6] One of the distinctive features of theological reflection, as the Whiteheads describe it, is that theological positions are formulated in conjunction with the pastoral situations in which they are to be put into practice. As a result, the pastoral response emerges from a particular context of ministry as it is theologically interpreted.

The variety of ministerial contexts that utilize this style of theological reflection is illustrated in the last section of the Whiteheads' book, where they invite four authors to share their experience and insights. The contexts for theological reflection that are discussed are adult learning, health ministry, Hispanic women and the church in China.[7]

Type of Experience

Obviously the type of experience that the Whiteheads use in their style of theological reflection is ministerial, but in a sense that may not be completely obvious. First of all, ministerial experience is not confined to the minister. The Whiteheads consistently draw attention to the wider circle of persons involved in any ministerial decision, and their examples typically reflect the setting of a parish or community of faith. As they emphasize in their introduction (xiii–xiv), a ministerial style of theological reflection is a corporate task.

Second, ministerial experience refers not only to the factual data of events that can be logically described and analyzed; it also refers to the extrarational data of feelings, convictions and insights that people of faith bring to the event and that become elements of its objective data.[8] Ministerial experiences are not impersonal cases to be analyzed; they are human phenomena calling for theological interpretation.

Third, the ministerial experiences used for theological reflection are concrete events in particular communities of faith rather than generic human experiences. It is one thing to reflect in general terms on the concept of human mortality or the dignity of the human person; it is quite another to reflect on the unexpected death of a teenager in the parish or the violation of workers' rights in the county. A ministerial style of theological reflection is more at home in the latter rather than the former type of experience.[9]

Fourth, in every ministerial experience there are overt, easily acknowledged factors and hidden, unrecognized or suppressed factors. Sometimes the latter exert greater influence on the meaning of a given ministerial experience than the former. One of the benefits of doing theological reflection in a group rather than privately is that these hidden dimensions are more likely to be uncovered. For the same reason a detailed, comprehensive account of the experience is necessary for engaging the whole experience, not just the parts that are pleasant and agreeable.

Finally, not just any ministerial experience is selected for theological reflection. The specific type of ministerial experience that the Whiteheads have in mind is an urgent concern or pressing issue, something more, therefore, than business as usual or the routine fulfillment of pastoral duties. Preferably such an experience is shared by the faith community as a whole, or at least by a significant portion of it.

What makes these ministerial experiences theological? They are theological because they are "the activities of *believing people* [sic], people formed within and by a particular religious heritage."[10] People who are already part of the faith tradition bring their experiences, ideas, beliefs, feelings and preferences to the situation. Theological meaning is imbedded in ministerial events, not because a minister is involved but because people of faith are involved, and their experience of the faith helps constitute the nature of the ministerial experience itself.[11] Each ministerial event is a microcosm of the whole faith tradition; it is partial and particular to be sure, but real and inviting nonetheless. It is that invitation which is key—an opportunity to enter the tradition more fully from the perspective of this ministerial experience and to enlighten and enrich this experience with the resources of the tradition. This perspective also explains the connection between ministerial experience and theology.

Connection to Theology

The pastoral concerns and issues in a particular ministerial experience furnish the agenda for theological reflection; they also provide the criteria for determining which resources in the faith tradition are relevant to the ministerial experience. In the Whiteheads' approach the whole of the faith tradition is available for theological reflection. There is no predetermination of sources or themes, although most reflectors turn instinctively to the Bible, and themes such as sin, grace, salvation, incarnation and community typically arise in ministerial experience. The point is that the experience itself provides the connection to theology. What it evokes is what theological reflectors should attend to. This is what distinguishes the form of theological reflection from the form of applied theology and other theological disciplines.

For the Whiteheads, engaging the tradition from the perspective of ministerial experience means that sometimes the pastoral perspective confirms the tradition, sometimes it clarifies aspects of it, sometimes it challenges it and calls for change. Conversely the tradition can confirm the meaning of a ministerial experience, clarify overlooked or hidden aspects of it, challenge people's attitudes and actions and call for change.[12]

The manner of conversation in this engagement is not polemical but assertive; the skill needed is not mastery but intimacy, a befriending of the sources of faith. How this works is illustrated in the Whiteheads' book by a chapter on the use of scripture.[13] Theological reflectors grappling with a pastoral situation typically look to the Bible for paradigms, images, themes and historical precedents that seem to correspond to the current concern or issue. These parallels are cited not to provide ready-made answers but to give testimony about how God has been experienced previously and how God's people have responded to that experience.

In the first stage there is a free association of possible points of contact between experience and scripture. This is followed by a more critical examination of those texts that seem to have the most relevance to the pastoral situation. This examination includes at least a literary and historical analysis (with the aid of commentaries) and possibly also an awareness of liturgical, moral and devotional uses of the chosen biblical passages. Wrestling with these meanings and implications leads to a sense of what the ministerial experience means biblically and what course of action it calls for.

Intended Praxis

The praxis envisioned by a ministerial style of theological reflection is a pastoral response to the issue or concern that initiated the reflection in the first place. Because this concern is rooted in concrete circumstances, these circumstances comprise the setting in which insights arrived at through the attending and asserting stages are translated into action. In this way continuity is maintained among experience, reflection and action. However, making the transition to praxis is not always easy or comfortable.

First of all, not everyone in a reflection group may agree on the same course of action, even if they concur with the analysis of the problem. Coming to a joint decision to act requires skill in consensus building, and sometimes conflict management.

Some may feel that arriving at a theological conclusion is all the action that is necessary, or they may feel the need for more information, more analysis, more assurance before deciding how to act on their theological convictions. Unfortunately, pressing pastoral concerns often call for action in the face of incomplete information, conflicting facts and inconvenient timelines. In any event, moving to action requires skill in planning and motivation.

Perhaps the greatest challenge in moving from insight to action is to insure that the intended praxis actually flows from and expresses the preceding theological reflection.[14] Sometimes reflection points toward a type of action that feels threatening or risky, and participants may opt for a response that is less consistent with their reflection but more compatible with their feelings. On the other hand, because members of a reflection group bring their prior experience and convictions to the issue, they can jump ahead to action and use theological reflection to rationalize what they want to do. Formulating a pastoral response that actually results from theological reflection requires the skills of coordination and logic.

The Whiteheads' ministerial style of theological reflection honors the complexity, ambiguity and pluriformity of real-life experience, including ministerial experience. By identifying the relevant sources of information and encouraging a mutually assertive conversation among them, they set up a process that virtually requires group reflection and better lends itself to making decisions regarding large-scale issues and long-term planning than to formulating pastoral responses to immediate crises.

3
A Spiritual Wisdom Style
of Theological Reflection

A spiritual wisdom style of theological reflection is rooted in the everyday life experiences of believing people. This style has a close affinity with catechetical and faith formation processes, but the term *spiritual wisdom* expresses better the meaning of theological reflection in this context. This is especially true for the works of Thomas Groome and the jointly authored book of Patricia O'Connell Killen and John de Beer.

Thomas Groome published his initial major work, *Christian Religious Education,* in 1980, the same year the Whiteheads published *Method in Ministry* (see chapter 2). He expanded and advanced the key ideas in that book with *Sharing Faith* in 1991. I will rely on the latter text for the discussion in this chapter.[1]

In 1994 Patricia O'Connell Killen and John de Beer published *The Art of Theological Reflection,* a distillation of their work over several years, helping persons connect their faith and daily life experience.[2] In the short time the book has been available it has become a welcome guide for programs ranging from adult education to spiritual direction and from ministerial training to community discernment.

Before examining the theological reflection style of these authors, it is important to say a word about the term *spiritual wisdom* (or *sapiential theology*). Spiritual wisdom refers to the original meaning of theology, as described by Edward Farley in his account of the development of theology and theological education.[3] In contrast to the medieval and modern understanding of theology as a system of doctrines taught by scholars and learned by students in an academic setting, *theology* originally meant "the wisdom proper to the life of the believer." This definition carries two implications: (1) faith is not just religious emotion or feeling; it is also a kind of knowledge; and (2) faith-knowledge is a practical sense of how to exist in the world before God (hence, it is spiritual). This spiritual wisdom is embodied in the tradition that the faith community hands on, but the believer's appropriation of it always occurs in the contemporary setting of the believer's existence.[4]

The authors in this chapter frequently and explicitly place their methods within the tradition of spiritual wisdom, even if they also use other terms to describe their work. The approach to religious education that Thomas Groome has developed and the process of reflecting theologically on everyday experience that Killen and de Beer propose fit the meaning of spiritual wisdom and represent a distinct style of theological reflection.

Groome's Shared Christian Praxis

Mindful that religious education has traditionally been limited to cognitive learning about the faith, Thomas Groome stresses from the outset the integral connection between knowledge and being (and uses a number of ancient and unusual terms to convey this perspective). What a person learns affects who a person is, and who a person is influences what a person learns. This conviction leads Groome to search for an "epistemic ontology," a way of knowing and learning (epistemology) that arises from and contributes to the being (ontology) of a person.[5]

The ultimate goal of an epistemic ontology is to enable people to consciously direct themselves as agent-subjects toward the realization of their being in relation to other people and the world. Groome calls this drive *conation*. Derived from a Latin word, it signifies a dynamic, striving movement of the whole person toward the satisfaction of the deep, human drive to become fully human. When this impulse is put in the context of Christian education, it refers to the informing, forming and transforming of people as disciples of Jesus shaping their lives in harmony with the reign of God. In this sense conation is synonymous with the notion of wisdom in Jewish and Christian tradition and with the general form of theological reflection insofar as "such wisdom arises from reflection on one's own life, from dialogue and the example of other 'wise' people, and from reflection on God's wisdom revealed through scripture and tradition."[6]

For Christian education to contribute to this basic human drive, it needs a conative pedagogy. In general terms such a pedagogy tries to do five things. It engages people in their complete self-identity, that is, all the dimensions of a person's makeup (corporeal, mental, volitional). It engages the place where people exist—the sociocultural setting of their lives. It engages people's sociocultural existence in dialogue with the historical tradition of the Christian community. It engages the dynamic structure inherent in the human striving for self-transcendence. It engages people in making decisions that enable them to appropriate the Christian faith as their own, as "living" faith. Concretely, these goals are accomplished through a method of shared Christian praxis, which describes Groome's style of theological reflection.

The method of shared Christian praxis begins with a focusing activity that leads to five sequential movements.[7] The focusing activity is an exercise designed to turn people toward their present praxis (their activity, life experience) and help them identify a "generative theme" (for example, reconciliation) within that praxis that has import and meaning for their lives. The focusing activity, and the theme it entails, may be part of the learning experience (reading a Bible story together), or it may occur outside the learning experience (as in a field trip); it may be a symbolic expression (the story of a saint) or a concern that people already share (parents for their children); it may be overtly religious (sacramental worship) or broadly human (concern for the elderly). The art of a religious educator is to determine with each group of learners the most effective type of focusing activity.

The theological rationale for this focusing activity, and for the whole process of shared Christian praxis, is the twofold conviction "(a) that God is actively revealing Godself and will in the everyday history that is people's lives in the world, and (b) that people are agent-subjects within events of God's self-disclosure and can actively encounter and recognize God's revelation in their own historicity through reflection on their present action in the world."[8] This is how people appropriate God's revelation in Jesus and make it their own—through their contemporary experience. Accordingly, the generative theme (reconciliation) emerging from the focusing activity becomes the nucleus of the learning experience and the focus of the five movements to follow.[9]

A Five-Movement Process

The first movement calls for participants to name or otherwise express their experience of the generative theme identified in the focusing activity. They may do so in reference to their own lives or the society around them or both. The expression may be verbal or nonverbal, religious or secular. It should be free of judgment or interpretation by others because it represents an honest statement of how individuals actually experience the common, generative theme. The rationale for this movement is grounded in the realization that God's revelation calls each person to be an agent-subject responsible for his or her personal and social life.

The second movement engages participants in a critical reflection on their experience of the generative theme as they expressed it in the first movement. The reflection may include an analysis of the past that has led up to the present action; a critique of current assumptions, interests, prejudices and values associated with it; a creative imagining of how the future might develop from present praxis. In this second movement participants shape their own stories and visions in a more reflective manner. This should help them clarify what God may be revealing through the present action or experience.

The third movement makes the Christian Story and Vision accessible to participants after they have reflected on the generative theme in the second movement. Story and Vision are metaphors that signal all the ways Christians have embodied the content of their faith (Story) and its promises and demands for their lives (Vision). Story/Vision does not refer to a single, normative expression of faith but to the accumulation of all the expressions bequeathed to succeeding generations by Sacred Scripture and Christian Tradition. This comprehensive resource sheds light on present praxis and enables participants to recognize God's self-disclosure in their own experience.[10] It also balances the personal testimony in movement two with the fund of community wisdom contained in the Christian Story and Vision.

The fourth movement engages participants in a dialectical hermeneutics that flows between their own stories and visions and the Christian Story and Vision. The dialectic pivots around questions such as: How does the Christian Story/Vision affirm, question and call us beyond present praxis? How does present praxis affirm and critically appropriate the Story/Vision made accessible in movement three? The intent is to enable people to appropriate Christian identity by making "the faith" their own. This movement is based on the conviction that people have a natural capacity to make such connections between life and faith and to act on them.

The fifth movement fulfills the promise of the fourth by encouraging participants to decide how to live their Christian faith in the world. The decision may concentrate on any aspect of a person's living (cognitive, affective, behavioral) and be carried out at any level of a person's relating (personal, interpersonal, social/political). The rationale behind this movement is that

God's revelation occurs in deeds as much as in words, and the more persons of faith consciously enact what they know, the more aware they are of God's ongoing revelation. For this reason, shared Christian praxis is a cyclical dynamic, bringing life to faith and faith to life in an ongoing (and life-long) process.

Groome often emphasizes that the movements of shared praxis can be combined and enacted in a great variety of ways; it is not a lockstep process. To demonstrate the versatility and applicability of shared Christian praxis, he relates it to the pastoral ministries of liturgy and preaching, justice and peace, and pastoral counseling. Groome concludes with his personal creed as a religious educator, which may also be read as the spiritual wisdom he has gleaned from shared Christian praxis.

Killen and de Beer's Framework for Theological Reflection

In *The Art of Theological Reflection* Patricia O'Connell Killen and John de Beer define theological reflection as:

> the discipline of exploring individual and corporate experience in conversation with the wisdom of a religious heritage. The conversation is a genuine dialogue that seeks to hear from our own beliefs, actions, and perspectives, as well as those of the tradition. It respects the integrity of both. Theological reflection therefore may confirm, challenge, clarify, and expand how we understand our own experience and how we understand the religious tradition. The outcome is new truth and meaning for living.[11]

Although the framework Killen and de Beer propose for doing this is set within a Christian context, it could function in any religious tradition. In fact, like Groome, they pattern their style of theological reflection on the way people naturally think about their life experiences, which they describe as a movement toward insight. The image of a movement toward insight and the theoretical underpinning for it are derived from the work of

Bernard Lonergan, although his system of thought and key insights are not formally presented in the book but rather are incorporated in a less technical, more accessible way.

The movement toward insight undergirds Killen and de Beer's style of theological reflection. It facilitates an exploration or discovery of the ways God appears (is revealed) in the events of people's lives. The movement is stymied by the self-defeating standpoints of certitude and self-assurance. The former latches on to one expression of the faith as the only norm and tries to fit every experience into it; the latter eschews authoritative determinations altogether and relies only on personal experience and interpretation. Neither achieves the personal maturity and integrity that theological reflection and spiritual wisdom aim at. These come as gifts in the process of bringing life experience to the wisdom of the Christian tradition from the standpoint of exploration.

The movement toward insight begins with an experience that catches one's attention and engages one's feelings. To explore the meaning of such an experience, it is necessary to reenter it, typically through a narration of the event, which should be given without judgment or interpretation, without saying what the event means or why it holds that meaning. Such a determination is premature and at this stage would undercut the movement toward insight.

The narrative reentry puts a person in touch with the feelings aroused by the experience. These feelings are an important clue to the meaning of the experience.[12] Because of their importance, feelings should be named as accurately as possible even when they are powerful, disturbing or unexpected. When this is done, the feelings often suggest an image that symbolizes the experience and expresses the question, value or insight embodied by the experience. An effective image invites a person to explore it creatively and from different angles in order to gain insight into the meaning of the experience. Such insights usually contain implications for action that a person or group may put into practice if they are willing.

A Four-Step Movement

This general description of the movement toward insight provides the conceptual structure for Killen and de Beer's style of theological reflection.[13] The first step is the same: to focus on some aspect of experience. Here Killen and de Beer expand the concept of experience by identifying four sources or categories of experience: action or lived narrative (the stories and events of people's lives), tradition (the authoritative wisdom of one's religious heritage), culture (the symbols/values, structures and ecological environment of human groups) and positions (the attitudes, opinions, beliefs and convictions that a person consciously holds and is willing to defend).[14]

The second step also parallels the movement toward insight: let feelings lead to an image. Here Killen and de Beer use the feeling/image combination to identify the heart of the matter, "the central question, tension, issue, theme, problem, or wonderment of an experience."[15] For theological reflection purposes it may be helpful to state the heart of the matter in explicitly theological terms without, however, losing the affective energy conveyed by the feelings/image of the experience itself.

Neither of the first two steps needs to be explicitly theological. However, if one of the chosen sources of experience is religious tradition or if the heart of the matter is a religious issue, the process already has a theological character. Be that as it may, the third step is theologically decisive, for this is where the heart of the matter in the experience is correlated with the wisdom of the Christian tradition.

This correlation is intended to be a give-and-take exchange, comparing, contrasting, testing, developing and extending points of contact between experience and tradition. Through this interaction, a person hopefully comes to insight. The insight may confirm and deepen what a person already believes; it may offer a different perspective on the person's life and experience; it may propose a genuinely new direction for living. Any of these positive results can be frustrated by habits of interpretation that are not open to change or by the assumption that tradition consists of fixed, timeless truths to be applied to daily life without adaptation (the same sorts of obstacles noted by the Whiteheads in chapter 2).

Genuine insights—new ways of understanding, feeling, relating and acting—impel a person to put them into action, but this does not happen automatically. In fact, many people feel a certain inertia or reluctance to translate their insights into action.[16] To aid this phase of the process, Killen and de Beer recommend prayer, planning and the support of other people.

To illustrate their approach further, the authors provide nine examples of how people can reflect theologically, beginning with any of the four sources of experience. The goal is to help people recognize when and how theological reflection may happen spontaneously and to facilitate its happening methodically. Like Groome, Killen and de Beer encourage the designing of theological reflection exercises to help people develop the skill of reflecting theologically and acquiring the spiritual wisdom they seek.

There are many similarities in the style of theological reflection proposed by Thomas Groome and Killen and de Beer. Both styles are holistic, embracing the whole person in the person's whole context. Groome analyzes this in more detail philosophically while Killen and de Beer address it through their expanded fourfold notion of experience.

Both are dynamic, using the image of movement to convey their process of theological reflection. For Groome, shared Christian praxis entails five movements heading toward the reign of God; for Killen and de Beer the framework for theological reflection is a modification of the human movement toward insight.

Both are confident in their use of life experience for theological reflection and base it on a theology of revelation that Groome pairs with each of his five movements more explicitly than Killen and de Beer do with theirs. However, both insist that attention to personal and group experience should be balanced by the faith tradition so that theological reflection does not become overly individualized but remains a form of spiritual wisdom.

Both develop their approach in harmony with the natural way people think and learn. For Groome, this leads to a conative pedagogy; for Killen and de Beer, to the movement toward insight.

Both advocate a reciprocal correlation between experience and Christian tradition, understood in a full, inclusive sense, although Groome asserts a more dialectical edge in his approach.

Both envision the praxis of faith as the outcome of theological reflection, but Killen and de Beer describe it in more provisional terms than Groome does.

Type of Experience

The type of experience suitable for a spiritual wisdom style of theological reflection is any life experience which arouses interest or feelings by suggesting a deeper meaning that is important for one's relationship with God and others. Obviously this is a very broad understanding of experience. Groome tries to concretize it by referring to the cognitive, affective and behavioral dimensions of human existence; Killen and de Beer try to concretize it by specifying four sources of experience (lived narrative, religious tradition, culture and personal positions).

Regardless of how they are categorized, experiences with potential for spiritual wisdom occur all the time, but most people are not aware of them. One of the purposes of this style of theological reflection is to enable people to pay attention to what is going on in their lives. To achieve this, Groome as well as Killen and de Beer base their methods on the way most people naturally reflect and learn, and they design exercises and initiate activities to help people recognize what is theologically meaningful in their lives.

Although a specific type of experience is not predetermined (as it is in the ministerial style of theological reflection), a specific representation of experience is sought. For Groome it is a generative theme; for Killen and de Beer it is the heart of the matter. For both this becomes the point of contact between lived experience and the faith tradition.

What makes experience theological for both approaches is the inclusion or insertion of explicit theological material into the experience (as it is represented by the generative theme or the heart of the matter). For Groome this occurs when the Christian Story and Vision are made accessible to the story and vision of the participants; for Killen and de Beer it occurs (most fully) when the heart of the matter is correlated with the sources of Christian tradition, especially scripture and doctrine. Neither conveys the impression that experience is inherently, or at least evidently, theological. Both recast the experience (through a generative theme or a feeling-induced image) to make it theologically conversant.

At the same time both Groome and Killen/de Beer affirm an understanding of revelation as God's ongoing disclosure to human beings in and through the events of their lives. This means that believers should have some sense of God's self-disclosing presence in their experience (akin to the Whiteheads' assumption that believers in a ministerial situation partially constitute the situation with/through their faith). The purpose of shared Christian praxis and the fourfold framework for theological reflection is to help people translate their general sense of God's revealing presence into a more concrete, definite experience of that presence. The experience is potentially theological because of God's revealing presence in it; it is actually theological (and becomes an expression of spiritual wisdom) when believers recognize and affirm that presence.

Connection to Theology

As with the ministerial style of theological reflection, no single theological source is preselected or required. The whole of the faith tradition in all its expressions is available for discovering meaning or coming to insight. What is distinctive in this approach is the way the faith tradition is entered or accessed. For Groome this happens through the stories and visions of the learners; for Killen and de Beer it happens through the images that people's feelings suggest.

For both views (as for that of the Whiteheads) the engagement with tradition is interactive. Groome uses the language of dialectical hermeneutics to describe this, but he does not mean the classic dialectics of Hegel and Marx. His understanding is more of a developmental give-and-take that advances by incorporating previous insights into new positions rather than rejecting the previous for something wholly new. Killen and de Beer speak in terms of a correlation that can confirm, modify or change the meaning of a person's experience or the person's understanding of the faith tradition. In either case correlation implies a creative synthesizing of old and new as people move toward insight and new horizons of meaning.

Intended Praxis

All three authors affirm the practical outcome of their reflection style, although Killen and de Beer describe this more provisionally, that is, an insight "may" prompt persons to action if they are willing. Groome is more insistent that the whole purpose of the reflection is to shape praxis—though broadly defined as cognitive, affective or behavioral action. Killen and de Beer may be more realistic about how often and how well this happens. In the same vein, they are more alert to the obstacles that prevent persons from translating insight into action and offer suggestions for overcoming them.

Overall these representative authors of a spiritual wisdom style not only pattern their theological reflection on natural human ways of knowing and acting, but they also exhibit great confidence in this natural process, trusting it to carry people to deeper meaning and to a genuine relationship with their faith heritage if they become aware of it and learn to use it.

4
A Feminist Style of Theological Reflection

A feminist style of theological reflection is a collective enterprise with many voices throughout the world contributing to the whole rather than one or two first-world authorities defining and dominating the field. To be sure, there are major representatives whose names and work are synonymous with feminist theology (such as Mary Daly, Rosemary Radford Ruether and Elisabeth Schüssler Fiorenza), but from the perspective of theological reflection methodology, a feminist style is an international, collaborative undertaking.[1] For this reason the present chapter relies on published surveys, overviews and collections of feminist theological reflection rather than a detailed summary of one or two authors.

The collaborative style of feminist theology is reflective of its comprehensive and interlocking purpose—to liberate the whole human community, especially the poor, in harmony with the earth from restrictive and destructive social structures and policies. As such, it is the most fully articulated expression of liberation theology in North America, but it is not simply concerned with the liberation of women. It also aims at the liberation of men and the freeing of the earth from exploitation.

Feminist theology is genuine theology, but it is not a separate discipline or branch (as might be suggested by terms like "women's

27

studies" or "women's issues"). It embraces all theology and examines each of the established disciplines with regard to its assumptions, foundations, history, conclusions and possibilities. Feminist theology is rooted in women's experience, but it recognizes the diversity of that experience as exemplified by the emergence of *mujerista* and womanist theologies (referenced in the next chapter). Feminist theology focuses on theological issues, but it is part of the larger societal effort to overcome sexism and to structure society on the basis of mutuality and equal regard. To address such a wide-ranging and complex agenda, a feminist style of theological reflection is necessarily a collective enterprise.

For the most part feminist theologians have not spelled out a method of reflection in the detailed, step-by-step manner of the other authors reviewed in this book. Theologian Anne Carr suggests why. Noting that feminist thinkers have been engaged in a variety of topics over several decades, she comments: "Perhaps it is only after such wide engagement, when there is a substantial body of material, different ways have been tried, and the results assessed, that the more theoretical issue of method can be fruitfully explored."[2] Be that as it may, Carr's description of the main stages of feminist theology corresponds to the standard movements of theological reflection.

First, there is a critical consciousness of the experience and condition of women everywhere in the world at the present time (equivalent to the starting point of attending to present praxis/experience). Second, this critical consciousness leads to a critique of the Christian tradition as interpreted from the perspective of women's experience (equivalent to the dialectical correlation of experience and tradition in theological reflection). Third, the critique of Christian tradition uncovers forgotten, devalued or suppressed examples of women and women's perspectives within the tradition itself, which are used to reinterpret Christian theology (equivalent to the formulation of new insights resulting from theological reflection). Finally, the reinterpretation of Christianity is translated into new proposals for understanding and praxis (equivalent to the practical enactment of theological reflection). Each of these steps warrants a fuller explanation.

Critical Consciousness

A feminist style of theological reflection begins with the harsh realization that women have experienced persistent oppression ranging from physical and emotional abuse to unequal pay for work and exclusion from certain roles in church and society. This has resulted in unnecessary depression, low self-esteem and a constant reminder that the way women are perceived and expected to function in the church and in society is not reflective of who they know themselves to be. This situation is not a mere discrepancy in points of view nor a difference of emphasis between men and women. It is a fundamental distortion of human relationships that pervades both church and society. And yet, because this pattern is so deeply imbedded and has been so long-lasting, it is not always easily recognized. For this reason, the first task of a feminist style of theological reflection is to raise the consciousness of both women and men to discern that the way things are is not the way they should be.

A feminist style of theological reflection raises this awareness first of all with women, not because they are to blame for their situation but because they are the primary victims and must be the primary agents for change. Although there is much greater awareness today of discrimination against women than there was when feminist theology first appeared, there is still need for consciousness raising among women because of the constant pressure they face to internalize gender-biased views of who women should be, what roles they should fill and how they should act.

Not all of this pressure comes from men, but men must also become aware of the ways that women's rights and dignity are violated. This awareness does not come easily, even for sensitive men, because they tend to assume that existing patterns are acceptable since they do not experience their negative effects as women do. After all, the status quo has been designed and maintained to benefit men. Without sufficient prodding, men are not likely to question the way things are, much less change them.

The stimulus for raising consciousness is women's experience itself, not in a narrow, introspective sense but in a collective, historical-critical sense. This is not only the starting point for feminist theology, it is also the norm or authority for critiquing tradition and developing alternative interpretations. Other styles of theological reflection place great importance on the role of experience, but none, except perhaps an inculturation style, gives experience such explicit normative authority. This status is not without problems or critics, even among feminists themselves, but two implications are already clear.[3]

Women who theologize from their own experience are not disengaged, neutral analysts of an objective body of information. They are deeply and personally involved in the theological process, not only because they are reflecting on their own experience (which is true for all styles of theological reflection), but because the end result of their reflection has such a decisive bearing on women's identity and potential for fulfillment. Whereas other styles of theological reflection build into their methods techniques for personally involving reflectors, a feminist style, like other forms of liberation theology, cannot help but be a personally engaging, advocacy theology.

The second implication is that women's experience is not monolithic or identical. There are significant differences among women based on class, culture, religion, race, economics, politics, education and history. For this reason it is now more appropriate and more commonplace for women to declare and theologize from their "social location" than to appeal to a generic woman's experience or idiosyncratic personal experience. Invoking social location preserves the richness, diversity and complexity of women's experience while preventing it from being transmuted into an abstract category, which can misrepresent the experience of women or represent it selectively (as male depictions of women have traditionally done).[4]

Despite the acknowledgment of differences among women, there are some common elements that most women recognize in their experience. The most important of these with regard to theological reflection is a condition of injustice that is variously described as being marginalized, excluded, oppressed, devalued, disrespected, manipulated, romanticized or controlled. The culprit behind this condition is sexism.

Sexism is not simply a pejorative term for the attitudes of men. It is a description of the erroneous assumption that men are inherently superior to women and that maleness is the norm for what is human for both men and women. Accompanying this sexist attitude is a tendency toward dualism, which divides and subordinates everything and everyone from a male perspective. The primary cultural expression of sexism is patriarchy and paternalism; the primary ecclesial expression is hierarchy.

In a benign sense, sexism might be taken simply as a distorted view of human relationships, like chauvinism, requiring confrontation and correction. But in a historical and existential sense, sexism has shown itself to be a social sin because it irrationally and unjustifiably obstructs the human flourishing of women while threatening to corrupt God's revealed truth and the nature of Christianity itself.[5] Awareness of these deep-seated implications leads to the second phase of feminist theological reflection.

Critique of Tradition

The unjust, sexist treatment of women is not a recent phenomenon. It is coextensive with history, and the tradition of the church is not immune from it. In fact, it has contributed to it, with negative assessments of women throughout history and with various restrictions on women's roles in different Christian denominations.[6] Because theological reflection always involves a correlation of contemporary experience with Christian tradition, it is imperative for a feminist style of theological reflection to uncover the sexist bias in Christian tradition in order to make truthful correlations. Of course, it is equally essential for other styles of theological reflection to take account of this bias, but it is an absolute priority for feminist theology.

To do this, most feminist theologians employ a hermeneutic of suspicion as they retrace and reread the Christian story (including its Jewish roots and multicultural contexts). This approach assumes that sexism has perverted the Christian message to some degree. The goal is to determine where and to what degree this has happened, and what implications it holds for the future. Although some feminist theologians have concluded that the tradition is totally corrupt and not salvageable, most work painstakingly at retrieving what stands up to their critical analysis. A feminist hermeneutic of suspicion is not, therefore, a cynical, reactionary dismissal of tradition; it is an honest, scholarly examination of the evidence, leading to the third phase of a feminist style of theological reflection.

Retrieval and Reinterpretation

The retrieval of Christian tradition by feminist theologians has taken two significant forms. The first is a piecing together of the actual situation of women that lies behind the extant records, including the New Testament. Perhaps the best-known practitioner of this type of retrieval is the biblical theologian Elisabeth Schüssler Fiorenza. In her decisive book *In Memory of Her,* Schüssler Fiorenza reconstructs the early Christian communities and persuasively argues that they were subversive models of egalitarian life in which women exercised full and effective leadership.[7] Her reading of scripture uncovers creative prototypes rather than changeless archetypes for future development.

While this kind of retrieval and reconstruction requires a certain degree of imagination, it is not fantasy or pure speculation. It is a careful reconstruction that demonstrates how a dominant patriarchal viewpoint has masked or suppressed contrary experiences, leaving clues nonetheless to an alternative vision and praxis. These hidden alternatives are not utopian possibilities; they belong to the tradition and are part of the full experience of the gospel. As such, they provide a basis for constructing alternatives to the present theology and praxis of the church.

The second form which hermeneutical retrieval has taken is the recovery of female perspectives and metaphors that have been neglected, subordinated, undervalued or forgotten in the course of male-dominated history. Unlike the previous example, these sources have not been suppressed; they simply haven't been utilized or given much attention. Once retrieved and made part of theological discussion, they provide a hitherto untapped resource for theological reflection and praxis.

One of the best-known examples of this type of retrieval is Elizabeth Johnson's trinitarian theology *She Who Is*.[8] Recognizing how the understanding of the Trinity has been cast in exclusively male terms, Johnson retrieves the biblical metaphor of Sophia-Wisdom to construct an understanding of the Trinity from a female perspective. To this end, she begins with a discussion of Spirit-Sophia that coheres better with women's experience and then discusses Jesus-Sophia and Mother-Sophia, drawing out rich implications for a relational and compassionate God.

In retrieving the tradition in either of these two ways, feminist theologians seek to reinterpret and reconstruct Christian theology. They are not simply adding a feminist viewpoint to existing theological positions or offering an optional perspective that one may choose to accept or not. The alternatives that a feminist style of theological reflection generates are intended to give the gospel a more complete and authentic articulation. Their proposals confront all Christians with a claim to truth that must be taken seriously. The scope of this task may be seen in the range of issues that feminist theologians address, extending from fundamental concepts of God, creation, sin, grace and salvation to specific concerns with prayer, morality, church and ministry.[9]

In formulating alternative interpretations, feminist theologians are also promoting a form of theological language that makes copious use of images, symbols, narratives and poetic expressions as well as art, music, dance and ritual. The word plays of Mary Daly *(gyn/ecology, methodolatry)* are complemented by the explicit language treatment of *Metaphorical Theology* by Sallie McFague. Double meanings like Mary McClintock Fulkerson's *Changing the Subject* are matched by the inverted meanings of titles like *Kiss Sleeping Beauty Good-Bye* and *Not Counting Women and Children.* More substantively, the imaginative language of feminist theology is intended to facilitate a more efficient transition from reflection to praxis, as exemplified by the promotion of ecofeminism, embodiment theology and women-church.[10]

Commitment to New Praxis

Given the starting point and hermeneutical assumptions of a feminist style of theological reflection, there is a deep commitment to change the church's current praxis. However, since true equality between women and men has not been the practice in Christian history, neither men nor women know ahead of time what this praxis will actually be like. It must be discovered as it is created, and it must be constantly evaluated in light of a hermeneutic of suspicion. A focal point in that evaluation is the meaning and use of power.

Power is the collective energy of women and men acting together. The key question is how power is exercised and for whose benefit. The goal of a feminist style of theological reflection is to use power in a participative way rather than a unilateral way and for the mutual benefit of women and men (and the earth that sustains them).[11] This is an immensely challenging task because there is scant precedent for it. What is clear is that a mere reversal of power (where women do to men what men have done to women) or an abdication of power (where women, and perhaps men, abandon the struggle altogether) will not satisfy the ideal of a new praxis.

Type of Experience

A feminist style of theological reflection obviously concentrates on women's experience, but with very specific connotations. First of all, it is the experience of women as victims of sexism. This already interpreted (or at least categorized) experience unifies women despite their other racial, cultural and societal differences and establishes the perspective from which everything else, including the Christian tradition, is interpreted. Second, women's experience of sexism is not simply women's. It also includes men who, as the perpetrators and beneficiaries of sexist systems, have a distorted experience of themselves and their humanity whether they know it or not. And third, women's experience of sexism is part of a more pervasive pattern of domination and control that threatens not only human relationships but the survival of the earth itself. Women's experience of sexism has an inherent connection with ecology that is not always recognized.

Perhaps the most distinctive and striking feature of women's experience for theological reflection is the intrinsic authority women give to it. Because sexism is so pervasive and because it is such a fundamental distortion of right relationships (sinful, in other words), sources of authority outside of women's experience are not immediately trustworthy; in fact they are all initially suspect. The critical feminist principle that Rosemary Radford Ruether initially articulated describes this situation: "...whatever diminishes or denies the full humanity of women must be presumed not to reflect the divine or an authentic relation to the divine, or to reflect the authentic nature of things, or to be the message or work of an authentic redeemer or a community of redemption."[12]

Of course, as noted earlier, women's experience is not a uniform reality, nor is it sealed off from the formative influences of a

sexist world. It too must be constantly scrutinized and clarified
(by women in dialogue with one another and with men) in order
to maintain the authoritative and trustworthy role it plays in a
feminist style of theological reflection. The international scope of
feminist theology is a great resource in this regard.

What makes women's experience theological is that it
exposes the one-sided, distorted view of the gospel that has been
handed on as normative, and it reveals more clearly and concretely
God's intention for human beings.[13] This is not a self-generated
intellectual exercise. In the very content of their existence women
embody a contrast experience through which the truth and meaning of the gospel are revealed anew. This represents a new source
of theological reflection. It provides a perspective for interpreting
Christian history that has not been employed until now, and it contains a wealth of insights and possibilities that have not been
expressed or developed in Christian tradition. In both respects, the
type of experience in a feminist style of theological reflection
holds enormous potential for change in theology.

Connection to Theology

A feminist style of theological reflection has a complex connection to inherited theology. It is not only critical in a scientific,
methodological way; it is also suspicious of sexist infiltration
even into the most normative texts and forms of Christian faith. It
is not only hermeneutical in the sense of interpreting meanings
that are there in the texts, practices and systems of tradition; it is
also hermeneutical in the sense of interpreting meanings that have
been suppressed and are no longer there but can be reconstructed.
It is not only speculative in the sense of developing doctrine; it is
also imaginative in the sense of formulating doctrine anew and
constructing alternative explanations of the faith. It is not only
concerned with "women's issues" in theology; it is concerned
with all of theology from women's points of view.

Throughout this critical-constructive interplay there is a

constant question about the validity and value of inherited theology. In what ways is it normative for subsequent theology (in the sense that feminist theology is accountable to it) and in what ways is it relevant (in the sense that feminist theology should deal with it at all)? The answers to these questions are being determined by the ongoing work of feminist theologians. That work suggests that a feminist style of theological reflection exhibits its own brand of nonfoundationalism because it cannot take for granted the normative claims of theological sources, including scripture and dogmatic pronouncements. The male-skewing of Christian faith in all its expressions precludes an easy assumption that the received tradition is the correct tradition and makes working with the tradition all the more complex and difficult.

On the other hand, this very awareness sets up the condition for a new kind of creativity. Precisely because it is assumed that the whole of Christian theology is tainted by sexist influences, the task is to construct alternatives and imagine how else the Christian faith might be expressed rather than simply correcting or modifying what has been handed down. In undertaking this project, feminist theologians have understandably given great attention to the nature and role of language.[14]

Language is not simply about ideas and words and forms of communication. Language shapes a worldview and influences the way people act and interact within it. For that reason, it is not simply a matter of changing a few offensive terms to satisfy a feminist sensitivity. Genuine alternatives must be created that open up a different worldview and describe how women and men act and interact when they share equal regard and mutuality for each other. Feminist theology, like all genuine Christian theology, is about living, not simply about thinking. For this reason a feminist style of theological reflection concentrates on language because it is both symbolic and formative.

In theology, language functions as a symbol pointing to and partially realizing what it speaks about. But the words are never fully the reality, even words like *God, Christ, grace, salvation* and *church.* Nor do any particular words exhaust the meaning of the reality. Other words, symbolic of other experiences, can always be substituted or added. If women's experience is a really new source of theological reflection, then it follows that new language is needed to express the truths of faith as women experience them. This would be true quite apart from the fact that current theological language is reflective of a one-sided (and oppressive) point of view.

Language is also formative. Words do not just convey ideas between minds; they depict the world (reality) in a certain way and they shape people's attitudes and behaviors accordingly. Inherited theology conveys a predominantly male worldview and way of functioning within it. Women see the world (reality) differently and want to create their own language for depicting it and describing how to function within it. Their suggestions for a new way of being together in a newly envisioned world constitute their intended praxis.

Intended Praxis

The intended praxis of a feminist style of theological reflection is emancipatory and transformative for both women and men, and the world that sustains them. Initially and most urgently, feminist theology is committed to the emancipation of women from male domination in all the ways that this occurs (emotionally, physically, intellectually, personally, financially, professionally, etc.). Secondly and implicitly, feminist theology is committed to the emancipation of men from a distorted and erroneous way of relating to women and the rest of the world. Thirdly and in concert with the first two, feminist theology is committed to the transformation of systems, structures, policies and institutions that perpetuate sexism and obstruct women's flourishing. Fourthly, but not least in importance, feminist theology is committed to the redemption of the physical world, to taking it back from the exploitative and irrational forces now draining the earth's resources.

This is an integrated praxis, each part affecting the others. It is a simultaneous, not a sequential strategy; it is holistic and inter-dependent. And it is not women's work alone. It is a collective enterprise and its success depends on the intrinsic persuasiveness of women's experience speaking for itself and for a new way of being.

5
An Inculturation Style of Theological Reflection

As the word *inculturation* suggests, the cultural setting in which people reflect on their experience is the main focus in this style of theological reflection; indeed, the cultural setting itself is the primary experience that people reflect upon. This approach, which frequently and intentionally uses the term *theological reflection,* has been developed most extensively by evangelizers and missionaries desirous of sharing the good news of Jesus Christ in cultural contexts that are not predominantly Christian.[1]

No one has articulated the issues involved in an incultura-tion style of theological reflection more perceptively or compre-hensively than Robert Schreiter. In this chapter I will rely on his two major books, *Constructing Local Theologies,* published in 1985, and *The New Catholicity,* published in 1997.[2] Other sources pertinent to the United States, especially those treating issues rel-evant to Hispanic/Latino and African American cultures, will be included in conjunction with Schreiter's analysis.

Schreiter's Local Theology

Local theology is Robert Schreiter's term for the effort of faith communities to construct their own interpretation of the gospel in relation to the cultural circumstances in which they live. He notes that "while the basic purpose of theological reflection has remained the same—namely, the reflection of Christians upon the gospel in light of their own circumstances—much more attention is now being paid to how those circumstances shape the response to the gospel."[3]

Schreiter identifies three models of local theology: a translation of one cultural expression of the faith (e.g., European) into the equivalent categories, if they exist, of another culture (e.g., African); an adaptation of one cultural expression into the philosophical worldview or indigenous framework of another culture; and a contextual construction that concentrates on the formation of cultural identity (ethnography) or the alleviation of oppression and social ills (liberation). While all three are rooted in gospel, church and culture, Schreiter affirms the contextual approach as the most fruitful and adequate.[4]

The need for local theologies has become more urgent in recent years for several reasons. New questions, such as the meaning and use of eucharistic elements in non-Western cultures, go unanswered by traditional theologies. Old answers tainted by colonialist, paternalist and racist assumptions don't ring true to new cultural experiences. And a new kind of Christian identity is emerging that begins with the cultural context, involves the community in developing a theological response to that context and recognizes how history has shaped the culture. This process of identity formation reflects the main features of the general form of theological reflection.

In *The New Catholicity* Schreiter sharpens this analysis. The need for local theologies has increased because of two factors: the universalizing tendency of established theologies and the effects of globalization. Although every theology is culturally contextualized, established theologies tend to universalize their positions, extending them beyond their own context to other cultural settings without honoring the distinctiveness and differences of those other settings.

The most outrageous example of this tendency in American history was the imposition of European theology and religious practice on the native peoples of the Americas during the colonizing period from the fifteenth century onward. An equally scandalous extension of this colonial theology was the capture and enslavement of Africans to develop the "new" world, a strategy that built into the culture a form of racism that has still not been eradicated.

Globalization entails a process similar to universalization. It represents the extension throughout the world of (European-American) modernity in politics, economics and communications. At the same time, this global extension of modernity has resulted in a compression of space and time, prompting local cultures to resist globalization by asserting their own particularity in whatever ways they can. Within U.S. culture this impulse toward resistance and self-assertion is found in both Black theology and Hispanic/Latino theology with their corresponding feminist versions of womanist and *mujerista* theology.[5]

The theological response to these universalizing and globalizing influences is a corresponding theological flow, a circulating movement of linked discourses that address the contradictions or failures of both cultural and theological global systems. In this respect a theological flow is an antisystemic movement. Current examples are theologies of liberation, which point to the failure of global economic systems to bring relief to the poor; theologies of feminism, which point to the failure of global systems to live up to the values of equality and inclusion of women; theologies of ecology, which point to the degradation of the environment; and theologies of human rights, which along with feminism point to the failure of global systems to reach the ideals of equality and inclusion for all people.

A different theological response to the impact of globalization is a cultural logic that opposes globalization altogether. Examples of this are fundamentalism and revanchism (reclaiming lost territory), ethnification (recovering a forgotten identity) and primitivism (returning to an earlier time period). While understandable, these responses do not engage the current cultural context and therefore do not represent an inculturation style of theological reflection.

A Map for Theological Reflection

As a guide for constructing local theologies (or developing an inculturation style of theological reflection), Schreiter offers a map rather than a method in order to avoid advancing the impression of a single, fixed way of proceeding.[6] The stimulus for developing a local theology may come from one of three sources: a confrontation with previous local theologies, the emergence of new cultural events or needs and developments in the larger church tradition.

Previous local theologies stimulate the construction of new local theology when the former are no longer adequate or become an obstacle to the community's development. In the United States this occurs when Hispanic/Latino, African American, or Asian American communities are expected to thrive by using the thought patterns and customs of a previously established and perduring Anglo-European theology. On the other hand, previous theologies do serve as a reminder of the local church's history and may even contain revelatory insights into the meaning of the gospel, as exemplified in elements of the *mestizaje* (mixed race) character of Hispanic life and the slavery spirituals and spirituality of African Americans.[7]

Ideally local theology begins with a careful listening to the culture in order to discover the Christ who is already active there. For example, the experience of a hyphenated and marginalized existence felt by many Hispanic/Latino, African American and Asian American communities has led to a deeper identification with Jesus as a "marginal Jew." In this respect, listening to the culture is like opening a text and paying attention to its themes. The themes, in turn, are most often determined by the identity and survival needs of the community and by the way things are done (or not done) in the culture.

When church tradition stimulates the construction of local theology, it usually entails a translation from one cultural context to another, that is, from the past to the present or from the culture of the headquarters (such as Rome, Geneva or Canterbury) to the culture of the local setting. To facilitate this translation, it is important to be sensitive to the cultural differences on both sides and to remember that tradition itself is a series of local theologies. This means that there is usually more diversity and more flexibility than the monolithic word *tradition* suggests.

Any of these stimuli sets in motion an encounter with church tradition; this is where the actual construction of local theology occurs. The key to this encounter is to identify parallels between the emerging local theology and the local theologies of the tradition. For example, there is a strong linkage in Black theology between the emancipation of African Americans from slavery and the exodus and exile experiences of Israel. Likewise Hispanics are very sensitive to the biblical parallel between the promised (holy) land and the land of their ancestors, now sectioned by artificial boundaries and controlled by colonial invaders.

An exploration of these parallels may lead to an affirmation of the local theology, a modification or even a correction, of it. At the same time the local theology may recall forgotten or avoided parts of the tradition, such as the complicity of Christians in colonization and slavery, a patriarchal bias toward women and children or an anthropological priority that neglects the environment. These painful memories can stimulate the further, positive development of the larger tradition through the contribution of its local theologies. Of course, the same sort of mutual influence can occur between a local theology and the culture in which it is constructed. Perhaps the clearest examples of this in the United States have been the local theologies of immigrants that helped make the labor unions successful in the early part of this century and the local theologies of African Americans that sustained the civil rights movement in the latter part of it.

Listening to Culture

As noted above, listening to the culture is the ideal starting point for an inculturation style of theological reflection. It avoids the condescending imposition of "what is best" from the outside and it maintains a proper openness and sensitivity to the local culture. In addition, listening to a culture should be holistic (taking the whole culture into account, not just select elements), attentive to the forces shaping identity within the culture and responsive to the forces that call for social change.

The typical ways of listening to a culture are functionalist (determining how the parts fit together to form the whole), ecological (determining how the society relates to its physical environment), materialist (determining how the physical environment affects the culture's worldview, needs and response to social change) and structuralist (determining the unconscious patterns that shape the culture). Schreiter identifies a fifth approach, semiotic, which he elaborates in detail.[8]

A semiotic approach to listening to culture examines the signs, messages and codes that express meaning in that culture. Because of the diversity within any culture, a semiotic approach relies on descriptions from different perspectives, among them inside-outside and speaker-hearer points of view. An inside description is usually a narrative that affirms the identity of the cultural group (e.g., Hispanic/Latino devotion to the *Virgin de Guadalupe* or an African American participative style of preaching). An outside description is usually also a narrative that explains and analyzes the same cultural experience. The cultural perspective of the speaker is rooted in concern for a clear transmission of the message (e.g., the church's theology of sacramental initiation). The perspective of the hearer is based upon relating the message meaningfully to the culture (e.g., integration of the sacraments with African initiation rites).

When these perspectives are brought to bear on culture texts, they examine identity (with special attention to group boundaries and worldview) and social change (with special attention to whether change is incorporated into the life of the culture or is a source of conflict with the culture). In every instance a semiotic approach analyzes the signs, messages and codes that express and convey, even enforce, meaning in the culture. Key indicators of this meaning are the metaphors (especially the root metaphors) used to describe meaning in the semiotic domains of the culture (religious, political, economic, sexual, etc.). For example, the cross is a root metaphor in the religious domain of Christianity, whereas the marketplace is a root metaphor in the economic domain of capitalism.

In *The New Catholicity* the process of listening to a culture is described as an intercultural hermeneutics, consisting of effective and appropriate communication between a speaker and hearers. In semiotic terms, the same message is communicated via different codes using a mixture of signs from two different cultures. Determining whether the same message is in fact being communicated has been the occasion for heated, and sometimes harsh, conflict within the church, as evidenced by the debate over Chinese rites in the seventeenth and eighteenth centuries, over modernism in the early twentieth century and most recently over liberation and feminist theology. Implied in the process of intercultural hermeneutics are always questions about the location of meaning, the nature of truth, the balance between difference and sameness and the active role of all the participants, especially the hearers or recipients of the message.

Obviously, listening to the culture as Schreiter describes it is a complex, demanding and creative undertaking. It goes far beyond narrating a single event in an individual's life or acknowledging the presence of cultural factors in a personal or communal theological reflection. An inculturation style takes the cultural setting of experience as the primary text and employs multiple tools to analyze and interpret it in order to stimulate a critical dialogue (dialectic) with the tradition.

Inculturated Theology

Turning to the faith tradition, Schreiter views it as a series of local theologies, which themselves are embedded in cultural conditions. Recognizing how different forms of theological thought are culturally contextualized helps to reappropriate the tradition for local theology and to facilitate a more adequate theological reflection (i.e., one sensitive to local cultural conditions). In general, theology has taken four forms of cultural expression.

The first is theology as variations on a sacred text. The variations may appear as a commentary (e.g., sermons), a narrative (e.g., lives of the saints) or an anthology (e.g., scholarly footnotes). The conditions that favor this type of theology are an oral (vs. a literary) culture and a focus on units of the text rather than the text as a whole.

The second form is theology as wisdom. Its scope is cosmic; its preoccupation is psychic-spiritual (i.e., the inner experience of human beings); and its logic is that of analogy. Theology as wisdom works best in a culture that has a unified sense of the person and the world, defines human growth as conformity to the unchanging patterns of the universe, stresses interiority and takes a two-level approach to ultimate reality.

The third form is theology as sure knowledge, that is, a reasoned, ordered account of the faith. This is the most common definition of theology, but it is not the most ancient and certainly not the only one. Theology as sure knowledge relates itself to other competing forms of knowledge, is devoted to analysis, builds systems of thought and is preoccupied with method. It functions best in highly specialized settings where there are competing worldviews (e.g., a university); it has a capacity for cross-cultural communication; and it thrives where analysis and explanation are needed.

The final form is theology as praxis, an analysis of social relationships and how they structure the social consciousness of a particular culture. Cultural conditions of oppression and injustice with the correlative goal of liberation foster this type of theology. Its main tasks are to disentangle true from false consciousness (ideology), stimulate ongoing reflection on social conditions and sustain the transformative praxis that is called for by theological reflection.

Schreiter makes clear that the construction of local theologies always occurs in dialogue with tradition, but this dialogue is not always smooth and certainly not one-sided. If the tradition can sometimes be paternalistic and insistent on perpetuating itself as normative (inviting resistance from the local culture), it also preserves a concern for unity and challenges the discontinuities and deficiencies of local theology.

Ultimately the goal of a local theology is to affirm Christian identity in relation to the immediate culture. Determining when this is the case is not a simple matter, but five criteria help (which Schreiter retains and nuances in *The New Catholicity*): (1) the cohesiveness of Christian performance, that is, how a local theology squares with scripture and church tradition; (2) the experience of the Christian performance in the context of worship and (3) in the context of the praxis of the community; (4) accepting the judgment of other churches and (5) a willingness to give judgment to other churches.

A valuable resource for constructing a local theology, out of favor until recently, is popular religion. Popular religion (or popular religiosity) has become a major factor in Hispanic/Latino theological reflection, although here too it was overlooked in the early stages (1950s and '60s) of this theology's resurgence.[9] Popular religion is often the best guide to what is most prized in the community's way of life, and it serves as an important reminder that culture is holistic, encompassing everything that goes into a community's experience.

A particular challenge for local theologies is the threat of syncretism and the coexistence of dual religious systems. In *The*

New Catholicity, Schreiter argues for a positive understanding of syncretism, virtually equating it with the synthesis of cultural elements that has always characterized Christianity and contributed to the formation of people's religious identity. This may occur through their resistance to negative cultural forces such as violence and exploitation, a hybrid combination of positive cultural elements or various forms of hierarchical influence (toleration, encompassment, legislation).

After assessing the future of contextual theology in Europe and the struggle of liberation theology with resistance and reconstruction, Schreiter situates the new catholicity in its historical context, arguing that the current period of globalization calls for a new wholeness. This wholeness respects the capacity of all cultures to receive and communicate God's Word with one another, recognizes that most people are compelled to experience culture in a fragmented and partial way (despite their desire for an integrated experience) and is characterized by a willingness to stand at the boundaries between those who profit and those who are excluded from the benefits of culture.

Type of Experience

The type of experience that an inculturation style of theological reflection addresses is, of course, cultural experience. But the precise meaning of cultural experience remains very elusive. In *The New Catholicity* Schreiter examines two broad concepts of culture—integrated and globalized.[10] Integrated concepts view culture as patterned systems yielding a unified whole. Theologically (as reflected in official church statements) this concept affirms the dignity of cultures, their ability to bring people to fulfillment and the right of people to their own culture. On the other hand, it does not respond well to dramatic changes in the culture, tends to limit the possibilities of inculturation and is ever fearful of syncretism.

Globalized concepts view culture as networks of communication through which symbols and patterns flow, beginning in a given region and eventually extending throughout the whole world. Theologically (as reflected in individual theological works) this calls for greater attention to moments of change rather than permanence, and attention to the asymmetries of culture (power, oppression) rather than the symmetries.

In either case, what makes cultural experience theological is the presumed presence of God's Word already in the culture—or at least the assumption that every culture has the capacity to give authentic expression to God's Word on its own terms. An integrated concept of culture presumes that the Word is already present in its patterns of culture which can be objectively known and, of course, always improved and developed; a globalized concept of culture presumes that the Word is present in the shifts and struggles of culture as it tries to construct itself in new and creative ways, not all of which can be known ahead of time or have historical precedent.

Connection to Theology

Despite the language of constructing theology and the advocacy of local communities taking the lead in doing so, an inculturation style of theological reflection is not an autonomous or rebellious undertaking. It is always in dialogue with the tradition. However, the tradition is understood as a series of local, culturally contextualized theologies rather than one overarching, supracultural theological norm. The point of connection is not the conformity of the local to the universal, but the recognition of common themes and patterns of Christian identity, which may take numerous, unexpected forms of expression. The open-endedness of this approach calls for something like criteria of verification rather than codes of strict compliance, and Schreiter supplies five such criteria.[11]

Because of the complexity of the cultural starting point, an inculturation style of theological reflection does not rely on a binary model of local initiatives and universal authority, but on the semiotic model of multiple signs and codes expressing a common message whose commonality is only known through its multiplicity. The outcome is not so much a self-contained local theology but a locally initiated, globally connected, pluralistically composed theological flow.

Intended Praxis

The intended praxis of an inculturation style of theological reflection is a more effective and appropriate formation of Christian identity and response to social change. These are not two separate goals but two phases of a reciprocal process. Formation of Christian identity does not take place apart from cultural influences, and Christian responses to social change should be guided by theological reflection on the culture, reflection that has a formative influence on those who engage in it.[12]

The goal is to recognize and utilize both factors. Intercultural hermeneutics, using a semiotic model of analysis, is an impressive way to do this. As with the other styles of theological reflection, there is no end result to the process in the sense of a final, complete system of thought or pattern of life. Rather there is a continuous theological flow fed by and contributing to the construction of local theologies as part of the ongoing tradition of the Christian life.

6
A Practical Style of Theological Reflection

A distinctive style of theological reflection characterizes the field of practical theology as it has been redefined and reoriented over the last twenty-five years.[1] Contemporary practical theology differs from its traditional counterpart in two important ways. It is a critical theological reflection on current praxis rather than an application of theory to practice, and it concentrates on the community of faith and its relationship to the larger society rather than concentrating on the pastor and the pastor's relationship to the congregation (commonly called the clerical paradigm).

One of the main leaders of this rejuvenated practical theology is Don Browning. In this chapter I will rely on his major work *A Fundamental Practical Theology,* published in 1991, and I will supplement it with reference to the more recent book *From Culture Wars to Common Ground: Religion and the American Family Debate* (1997), which he coauthored and which employs the method described in *A Fundamental Practical Theology.*[2]

Browning's Fundamental Practical Theology

From the outset of *A Fundamental Practical Theology,* Browning declares his conviction that all theology is practical, not

52

in the sense of applying theoretical knowledge to practical situations, but in the sense of interpreting the theory-laden practices of faith communities in order to make them more consistent and effective. In keeping with this conviction, Browning describes three different congregations, which he refers to throughout the book, to illustrate his understanding of practical theology. "I find it useful to think of fundamental practical theology as critical reflection on the church's dialogue with Christian sources and other communities of experience and interpretation with the aim of guiding its action toward social and individual transformation."[3]

Browning's understanding of practical theology is strongly influenced by the practical philosophy of Hans Georg Gadamer. Especially pertinent are Gadamer's starting point in human practice, his assertion that the fundamental structure of human understanding is dialogue or conversation and his insistence on the role of effective history, the influence of a person's preunderstandings and the dynamic of fusing horizons of meaning. The extension of Gadamer's thought to theology has been facilitated by David Tracy, whose revised correlational method Browning adapts and somewhat redefines for the purposes of developing a fundamental practical theology.[4]

Fundamental practical theology, as Browning defines it, investigates the conditions that make normative claims possible for the religious practices of faith communities. This process entails four movements.[5] The first is descriptive theology, which uncovers the religious meanings implied in the corporate and individual practices of both religious and secular communities. The second movement is historical theology, which investigates the effective history (a la Gadamer) of the normative claims underlying a community's practices. The third movement is systematic theology, which articulates (thematically) a new horizon of meaning emerging from the first two movements and establishes the validity of this new horizon.

These three movements culminate in the formulation of strategies for acting or what Browning calls strategic practical theology, the fourth movement. Strategic practical theology responds to four questions: How do we understand the concrete situation in which we must act; what should be our action (praxis) in this situation; how do we critically defend the norms of our action in this situation; and what means, strategies and rhetoric should we use in this situation?

The third question is especially important, and immensely challenging. It is not enough to analyze a situation and determine how to act in it; it is equally necessary to justify that action by defending the claims to validity that the action entails. Defending these claims does not require absolute certainty about the validity of specific actions, but it does call for an adequate defense in terms of the concrete situation.

Descriptive Theology

The starting point for a practical style of theological reflection is descriptive theology. The term *descriptive* might suggest a neutral, objective account of the situation being reflected upon. Browning forcefully disagrees with this assumption, proposing instead a hermeneutical approach that acknowledges the personal perspectives and preunderstandings of the describer(s) as well as the theology implicit in the practices described (hence the appropriateness of the term *descriptive theology*). The describer is not a disinterested observer on the outside looking in but an engaged participant in the midst of the situation. Consistent with this view, Browning was involved in various ways with each of the three congregations he describes and refers to throughout the book.

Because the lived situation is both the starting point and source of practical theological reflection, Browning advocates a "thick" description of the experience. To achieve this, he proposes a framework (previously set forth in his other works) consisting of five types or levels of input.[6] They are vision, obligation, human tendencies-needs, environmental-social setting and rules-roles. This schema is applicable to all four movements of Browning's method (descriptive, historical, systematic and strategic theology).

Levels of Practical Thinking

Vision designates a community's theological horizon, the set of ultimate religious meanings that they profess, such as their understanding of God, creation, sin, grace, redemption and salvation. These are the beliefs and values that define the community's identity and declare its stance in the larger social environment.

Obligations flow from the vision; they are the practical-moral implications for living out what is professed.[7] Obligations are not imposed externally or arbitrarily; they are a behavioral expression of the vision. When a discrepancy arises between vision and obligation (from either side), it sets into motion the process of practical theological reflection.

Tendencies-needs are the impulses shared by most people for food, shelter, security, relationships, self-esteem and the like. Although analysts of human growth and development such as Erik Erikson, Abraham Maslow and George Pugh have tried to identify universal human tendencies, it is notoriously difficult, if not impossible, to finally determine what these should be for all people. It is certainly helpful to have such general schemas available for reflection, but the tendencies and needs that practical theology is interested in are manifested in a community's concrete actions, responses, decisions and interpretations. These will change over time and between groups, affecting and sometimes altering a community's vision and sense of obligation. When this happens, it calls for practical theological reflection.

The environmental-social setting helps to shape a community's vision, obligation and tendencies-needs by determining the constraints on an otherwise idealistic picture. The social environment is not an ineffectual, empty context for human activity; it is part of the human reality. People living on the margins of social and economic prosperity, women in male-dominated societies, victims of ecological exploitation and warfare have a very different interpretation of human existence and Christian faith from that of their counterparts (people at the center, men, the exploiters) in those same situations. When a clash of perspectives within the same environmental-social setting occurs, it calls for practical theological reflection.

Rules-roles are the most specific determinants of human activity, spelling out who acts, in what circumstances, with what authority and by what means. As such, rules and roles contain their own implicit sense of vision and obligation, which may or may not be consistent with what a community professes or with the practices through which it responds to human tendencies-needs within environmental-social conditions. These discrepancies provide another occasion for practical theological reflection.

While descriptive theology may begin with any of these factors, it should begin with the one that is most immediate or pressing in the situation being described. However, for an adequate, "thick" description of a situation, all five should be taken into account. As general categories, they might be used for analysis from any perspective: philosophical, legal, social, economic, cultural or political. As tools for practical theology, they become explicitly Christian when they reveal the religious beliefs and theological understandings of a particular faith community and identify the issue that calls for theological reflection.

Historical Theology

Historical theology begins the critical reflection on the questions/issues surfaced by descriptive theology. It examines the normative texts that are already part of the effective history of the community—biblical teachings, confessional statements, doctrinal positions and community traditions. This examination is not a scholarly inquiry for its own sake; it is a reading of the texts with the practical questions/issues of the community in mind. Browning proposes his five-level framework as a helpful way to do this.

A community that has already described its situation in terms of the five levels can then compare its description with the vision and obligations that its normative texts contain, the tendencies and needs they address, the social settings that produced them, and the rules and roles they promote.

The community as a whole is expected to carry out this historical inquiry. When it does, there will undoubtedly be different levels of understanding and interpretation (what Browning calls levels of textuality). For this reason extended conversation must arrive at a consensus about the meaning of the classic texts for the current, practical situation. Once a consensus has been reached, it must be articulated and validated theologically. This is the role of systematic theology.

Systematic Theology

Systematic theology is essentially an exercise in normative thinking, a critical and creative dialogue between the theological positions implicit in current practice (surfaced by descriptive theology) and the theological positions implied in the normative Christian texts (sharpened by historical theology). The goal of systematic theology is to fuse a new horizon of meaning out of these positions. It does this by examining the general themes that current practice and normative texts share and then formulating a new interpretation that is responsive to the practical situation under consideration.

However, the task of systematic theology is not complete with this fusion of horizons of meaning. It must also supply reasons to support the validity claims of the new fusion, especially if practical theology is to engage in public discourse.[8] Typically establishing the validity claims of Christian praxis is the task of theological ethics, and Browning turns to Reinhold Niebuhr as his guide in filling in the Christian content of the fivefold schema. Each of the five levels contains claims that test the validity of new proposals: vision raises metaphysical claims; obligation raises ethical/rightness claims; tendency-need raises claims about human nature and premoral goods; environmental-social factors raise claims that constrain tendencies-needs; and rules-roles raise claims about concrete patterns of actual practice.

The end result of systematic theological reflection is not a foundational, objectively certain judgment but a set of sufficiently good reasons for acting a certain way. That course of action, formulated in broad conceptual terms, must be translated into practice. This is the role of strategic practical theology.

Strategic Practical Theology

Strategic practical theology (which Browning also calls fully practical theology because it completes the process and draws upon all the practical skills and activities of a community) is not the application of theological convictions to concrete situations as they arise. The practical concern has been operative throughout the process— in the description of the situation, in the analysis of historical, normative texts and in the fusion of horizons of meaning. Strategic practical theology is the intentional implementation of what practical theological reflection has been working toward all along.

In most cases, and certainly in the three congregations Browning refers to in his book, strategic practical theology involves education, pastoral care and transformation (change)—not only within the communities of faith but also in the larger society that they impact.[9] This is where the validity claims for the praxis decided upon are satisfied, and as the new praxis is enacted, it gives rise to new questions and issues that keep the practical theological process going.

Application to Family Life

Although Browning makes repeated and extensive use of the three congregations to concretize his method, a more sustained exercise of practical theology is found in the book *From Culture Wars to Common Ground: Religion and the American*

Family Debate. This work, part of a series on the family, religion and culture, addresses the crisis of families in the United States. Obviously this is not an issue confined to a single congregation or community. However, Browning (and the colleagues with whom he wrote the book) profile five American families who together exhibit most of the features of the current crisis and give the reflection a concrete, personal point of contact.

The book does not use the categories of descriptive, historical, systematic and strategic practical theology, but it moves through the same steps, referring to them as "issues, traditions, voices, and directions." The starting point is a description of the issues as they surfaced between 1990 and 1996. The overriding issue that is brought to critical reflection is the diverse understanding of love manifested in modern family life (i.e., from the nineteenth century to the present). Three competing images emerge: self-sacrificial love, self-absorbed love and equal regard/mutuality love.

The authors judge the third as the most adequate for families, but they examine the tradition with all three in mind. Specifically, they dwell on the views of Thomas Aquinas, because his naturalistic approach is accessible to all reasonable people, and on the position of Martin Luther, because his biblical-faith approach is congenial to Christian communities. At the end of their treatment of traditions, the authors confront and reinterpret those New Testament texts that seem to endorse a one-sided, father-as-sole-head-of-the-family position (Eph 5:23, Col 3:18, 1 Pt 3:1). This historical inquiry yields four conclusions: Christian love should point toward mutuality or equal regard; self-sacrifice is part of mutuality love, not an alternative to it; the concrete meaning of mutuality should be determined within the human life cycle; and families are subordinate to the larger common good viewed either as the reign of God or as the good of civil society.

These conclusions are put into dialogue with the contemporary voices (systematic reflection) of feminism, family therapies, pro-family movements and economics. The result is a fusion of horizons, which the authors call a "new critical familism and culture of marriage" based on full equality between husband and wife with a corresponding ecology of support for families.

This vision is given direction in the two ways required by strategic practical theology. First, a practical theology of families based on equal-regard love is articulated with validity claims drawn from philosophy (the shared rationality of men and women), scripture (equal regard of women and men in the eyes of God), psychology (mutuality in the human life cycle) and Christian theology (families within the reign of God). Second, this theology is translated into sixteen strategies of implementation—nine for use within congregations and seven for use by congregations within society. Each strategy is a behavioral expression of the practical theology constructed by historical and systematic reflection on the current practice of family life.

Type of Experience

The type of experience on which Browning's practical style of theological reflection focuses is both communal and problematic. It is the experience of communities of faith rather than that of individual members or their pastoral leaders which initiates practical theology. More specifically, practical theology is interested in the experience of communities as they practice their faith, whether this practice occurs within a congregation (e.g., worship, religious education, pastoral care) or as part of a larger social life (e.g., family crises in society, response to cultural influences, contributions to public policy). Because of this communal emphasis, practical theology requires a layered description of experience, not in a disinterested, neutral sense but in an effort to uncover the theological positions implicit in the practices.[10] Browning's fivefold schema is one way of trying to insure a sufficiently thick description.

A practical style of theological reflection is also problem oriented; it looks for the discrepancies, inconsistencies and inadequacies of current practice when compared with the values and ideals those practices are intended to implement. The source of the conflict may come from either the practical or the theological side, just as it may arise from within congregational life or in the relationship between a congregation and the larger society.

The clash between theory and practice in such situations does not imply a dualistic separation of the two, but it does pose the challenge of constantly bringing theory and practice into the best harmony that concrete situations allow. In this sense practical theology is not an occasional, problem-solving technique but an ongoing way of doing theology and living the Christian faith.

What makes experience theological in a practical style of theological reflection? Experience is theological because of the religious meanings and values implied in the practices of Christian communities. This hidden theological dimension is not confined to the practices of Christians. It is part of the interpretive framework of Western culture and comes to expression in the work of the human sciences. Here Browning agrees with social scientist Robert Bellah that "all social science perspectives...have hidden in the background not only pre-understandings and prejudices shaped by effective history but an effective history with religious dimensions."[11]

Practical theology focuses on these implicit religious dimensions in its description of situations and seeks to make them explicit and thematic. This is not the same as bringing religious meanings to a situation that is in itself devoid of such meanings; it is making directly and immediately available for reflection what is already there, albeit unrecognized and unacknowledged.

Connection to Theology

Practical theology is oriented to the full body of theological truth from the outset by looking for the theological meanings imbedded in the practices of communities of faith. The practical starting point always has a theological horizon; theological inquiry always has a practical outcome in view. The connection is never broken. Of course, some degree of theological knowledge is presupposed in order to recognize theological meanings within practice in the first place. While individuals may not have sufficient competence to do this, communities of faith do. This is another reason why practical theology is an exercise of communal discernment rather than private interpretation.

More formally, historical and systematic theology are the main dialogue partners for practical theology. The questions/problems surfaced by descriptive theology are taken to historical (normative) texts, primarily scripture and dogma, and are given a systematic (thematic) articulation. This is both a hermeneutical and a normative exercise. It seeks the meaning of historical texts in light of current praxis and the meaning of current praxis in light of historical texts. This interplay makes possible a fusion of new horizons with implicit claims to validity and truth. These claims must be tested and defended not just theologically but philosophically and humanly, not just in theory but also in practice. This is the task of theological ethics.[12]

In this respect, theological ethics is the pivotal connection between practical theology and the rest of theology. The practices that practical theology initially describes are human, moral actions more or less consistent with the religious and moral values the practitioners profess. After a critical examination of the theological meanings involved, new or altered practices may be proposed. Their effective implementation may depend on skills of communication, persuasiveness, planning, reinforcement, etc., but their validity, and ultimately the success of practical theology as theology, depends on the judgment of theological ethics.

Intended Praxis

The praxis intended by practical theology is twofold: praxis within a faith community and praxis by a faith community within a larger social setting. Although the emphasis may be on one or the other, the two are always intertwined. This is clear when Browning speaks of the goal of Christian education as both discipleship and citizenship, or when he argues that a critical new familism does not require Christian belief (with the possible exception of affirming the value of sacrificial love) although Christian belief deepens and clarifies its meaning.[13]

Ultimately the praxis of practical theology is transformational. It begins with a discrepancy between current praxis and belief, and it tries to overcome the discrepancy by proposing a more coherent theology and a more consistent praxis. It is not possible to know ahead of time all the changes this will require or who will be most affected by them. That is what the process of practical theology is for. But it is clear that change of some type will occur and will continue to occur as long as people try to put into practice what they believe.

7
Conclusion

What are theologians saying about theological reflection? Over the past twenty-five years, quite a lot. Not only do contemporary theologians stress the value and importance of theologizing from/with experience, but they also suggest how to do this.[1] Their suggestions fit the general form of correlating lived experience with the sources of Christian faith in order to practice that faith more effectively in real-life circumstances. This practical goal means that theological reflection is ultimately intended for every believer; it is not a theological specialty reserved only for experts.

Within the general form of theological reflection, distinct styles are recognizable: ministerial, spiritual wisdom, feminist, inculturation and practical. The most obvious distinguishing feature among these styles is the type of experience chosen for reflection; the most important distinguishing feature is the way they correlate experience with the faith tradition. Whatever else theologians have been saying about theological reflection and what more they need to say in the future may be grouped under three headings, corresponding to the main components of this general form of theologizing.

Experience

Proponents of theological reflection usually do not discuss the nature of experience in philosophical terms. They are content

64

to let experience stand for "what happens" in the life of an individual or community.[2] While this may give the impression that theological reflection is not intellectually sophisticated, it actually means that any experience can be reflected upon theologically. Obviously, some experiences are more suitable than others, and part of the task of theological reflection is to help people choose experiences wisely. How this is done deserves continued attention and suggestions from advocates of theological reflection.

The two types of experience most frequently selected are new, creative, positive events and problematic, disruptive, crisis events. The common element in these two extremes is the affective energy they stimulate. This means that theological reflection deals with nonrational factors (emotion, intuition, motivation, behavior) as much as rational factors, making it a more, not less, demanding exercise than typical intellectual work. Overall, the best experiences for theological reflection are those which signal that something meaningful is going on. Theological reflection directs itself toward this meaning and tries to express it in theological terms.[3]

Although meaningful experiences occur as engaging, energetic events, people do not always pay sufficient attention to them or enter them as fully as they might. Consequently, another important task for theological reflection is to alert people to their own experience and the potential theological meaning it contains (or reveals). This is variously described as attending to experience (the Whiteheads), focusing on present praxis (Groome), recognizing one's situation (Killen-de Beer), raising critical consciousness (feminists), listening to culture texts (Schreiter) or describing theory-laden practices (Browning).

The appeal to human experience is based on the assumption that it is not a spiritual void waiting to be filled with meaning from the outside. Either it already contains theological meaning or it has analogous elements that can be used to fashion a real (rather than a nominal or hypothetical) connection to the sources of Christian faith. At present, those who assert that experience has an inherent theological character tend to invoke as their rationale a theology of revelation or a theology of incarnational grace and redemption; those who assert that experience has an affinity to theology tend to look for parallels, common themes, similar issues and analogous insights between experience and theology. In the future, advocates of either approach will need to bolster their positions with more explicit theological arguments.

Since experience does not occur in the precise terms of formal theology, some sort of translation or representation of experience is needed for theological meaning to be recognized and affirmed. The standard technique for representing one's experience is to narrate it, orally or in writing, and usually to people who are prepared to reflect upon it theologically. This narration is expected to be a creative exercise, employing the imagination in order to reenter the experience and discover what it has to tell. However, narration is not interpretation. The former is a factual account of what happened; the latter is a personal account of what it means. Interpretation is the ultimate goal of theological reflection, but it takes a while to get there, and it requires a high degree of intellectual and emotional maturity to withhold premature judgments. Because the meaning of experience is rarely self-evident, it calls for examination, analysis, comparison and observation from different perspectives. In short, theological reflection relies on a critical awareness of one's experience.

Critical awareness means that reflectors do not just want to know what happened; they want to know why it happened this way rather than that. What difference did it make that these people rather than those were involved, that the event took place here rather than there, at this time rather than that? Critical awareness clarifies the conditions that make any experience what it is and sets the stage for an informed judgment about what the experience means.

Perhaps the most distinctive feature of theological reflection with regard to experience is the authority it has, functioning as both the source and criterion of theological meaning. As a source, it is either a concrete realization of God's revealing, saving presence in people's lives, or it is a reflection of the meaning of God's revelation and salvation as they have been discerned in Christian history. In both instances it is a theological source in its own right; it contains theological meaning as part of its reality. Exactly how this is so can always use more clarification and elaboration. What is clear is that the role of experience in theological reflection is quite different from its role in illustrating theological truths pedagogically/ homiletically or applying them pastorally.

As a criterion, experience provides the basis for determining the relevance and relative adequacy of any additional theological meanings correlated with it. This does not mean that experience determines what is theologically true and valid in itself or in relation to other experiences. Advocates of theological reflection must continue to make this clear lest theological reflection be falsely accused of promoting a subjectivist, relativist approach to Christian faith. Experience as a criterion simply means that theology must honor the concrete conditions and limitations of any given experience.[4] Not everything theology has to say is relevant to a particular experience, and no particular experience exhausts the full meaning of theology. This becomes more clear in the way experience is correlated with theology.

Theological Correlation

Proponents of theological reflection advocate a dynamic, reciprocal relationship between lived experience and the established faith tradition. This is signaled by the images of movement, flow or process that are typically used to describe the correlation of experience and tradition. At the same time these images should not suggest that the correlation is always a smooth, harmonious fit. Proponents of theological reflection speak just as often of a dialectical relationship and a critical correlation—and in the case of feminist and inculturation styles of theological reflection, a hermeneutics of suspicion.

To achieve the type of correlation it envisions, theological reflection encourages an assertive approach which questions, examines, explores and tests both the tradition and contemporary experience. The goal is not to attack the tradition, but to befriend it; it is not to dismiss the tradition, but to make it accessible. Achieving this type of engagement requires, once again, a high level of intellectual and emotional maturity. This is one reason why theological reflection occurs most fruitfully in a group or community where the shortcomings and limitations of individuals may be compensated by others.

The model for the reciprocal correlation that theological reflection advocates is a conversation or dialogue. This is usually proposed in the sense of a respectful openness to different viewpoints and the recognition of truth wherever and however it appears. Showing why this is a valid and beneficial way to appropriate the faith tradition is a task theological reflection must continue to address, especially in response to those who take their own experience as the sole norm of truth or those who insist on a rigid conformity to a previous formulation of the faith.

The critical correlation of lived experience with the faith tradition has yielded two significant types of results, best exemplified by a feminist style of theological reflection. One is a retrieval of overlooked, undervalued, or suppressed elements in the tradition; the other is a reconstruction of traditional teachings and practices through alternatives stimulated by contemporary experience. Both results manifest how pluriform, complex and ambiguous the tradition actually is.

Recognizing this can free people from feeling obliged to conform strictly to one particular interpretation of the faith, but it also raises questions about the criteria for verifying new formulations of the faith and corresponding practices. This is an issue which proponents of theological reflection have not yet sufficiently addressed. They have tended to rely on confidence in the process of reflection and to assume that the results would not conflict with the inherited meanings of the tradition. However, as feminist, inculturation, and practical styles of theological reflection do come into conflict with the tradition, the need for criteria of verification becomes more evident. And the search for those criteria is directed more toward the resulting praxis than theoretical or authoritative arguments.

Praxis

Practical concerns govern the theological reflection process from the outset. They are not simply the last step in a process that moves along independently until it turns its attention to praxis at the end. Practical concerns constitute the context within which theological reflection takes place. Although positive experiences arising out of daily praxis can always initiate theological reflection, most of the time the practical concern that sets the process in motion is a problem to be solved, a decision to be made, a crisis to be overcome, a need to be met, an inconsistency to be corrected, a wrong to be righted, a question to be answered, a dilemma to be resolved, a discrepancy to be clarified.

Because practical concerns initiate, contextualize and culminate each exercise of theological reflection, they provide continuity from one instance to the next and help insure that theological reflection will be an ongoing activity rather than an occasional, sporadic event. The pervasive presence of practical concerns also makes it more likely that theological reflection and the praxis resulting from it will be realistic. However, this is not a guarantee nor does it happen automatically—and it is the phase of the process to which proponents of theological reflection have given the least attention.

There are three critical issues involved in the praxis phase of theological reflection which must be addressed more fully in the future. The first is the conversion of ideas into behaviors. This calls for moving between two very different types of activity, and not everyone can do it well. Persons who can define issues abstractly and manipulate mental categories effectively are not necessarily capable of figuring out how to make things work in practice or even of recognizing the same ideas in practical circumstances. This difficulty is compounded when people who are trained academically, i.e., professional theologians, assume that they are doing the real work and that practical implementation is just a matter of carrying out ideas, which anyone can do.

The second critical issue with regard to praxis is closely related to the first. Every situation poses certain obstacles to effective implementation. Moving from reflection to praxis means anticipating the obstacles in a given situation and figuring out how to overcome them. This requires both a knowledge of the situation (which reflectors outside of it cannot know) and a sense of what works and how. All this is essentially a question of strategy and the skills it requires do not come automatically with insight into ideas.

The third critical issue flows from the second. Because praxis involves a translation of reflection into action, it is important that the action express the same meaning as the reflection (the hermeneutical and semiotic issue again). This is especially true when the praxis has a public character or intersects with the action and thinking of others who are not motivated by theological or faith perspectives. Behavior speaks its own language. What it communicates in a given situation is crucial to the praxis phase of theological reflection.

Regardless of how these issues are handled, theological reflection anticipates that every praxis will involve some type of change. This may occur at a personal, communal, institutional or societal/cultural level. Changes at the last level have far-ranging implications and the stunning impact of theological reflection by women, economically oppressed groups and cultural minorities can give the impression that theological reflection always aims at widespread, radical change. In fact, only experiences of sufficient magnitude are likely to result in such large-scale change, and those experiences are relatively rare.

More typically, theological reflection envisions incremental changes in the faith formation and Christian identity of individuals and groups. This usually takes the form of a more complete, personal appropriation of the gospel that has an indirect impact on other life settings. Of course, transformation of systems, policies and official practices is also always possible, but it is not the primary or only intended outcome of theological reflection. Rather, the goal of praxis is to realize what reflection makes possible. For theological reflection this is never determined ahead of time. It grows out of the originating experience, critically correlated with the faith tradition and skillfully put into practice. That's not just what the theologians are saying—it is also what the Christian faithful are doing.

Notes

1. Introduction

1. For a brief discussion of the historical background of the term *theological reflection,* see Robert L. Kinast, *If Only You Recognized God's Gift* (Grand Rapids, Mich.: Eerdmans, 1993), 1–3, and *Let Ministry Teach: A Guide to Theological Reflection* (Collegeville, Minn.: Liturgical Press, 1996), xi–xiv.

2. See David Tracy, "Traditions of Spiritual Practice and the Practice of Theology," *Theology Today* (July 1998): 235–41. For a more elaborate discussion of theology as form, see Han Urs von Balthasar, *Seeing the Form,* vol. 1 of *The Glory of the Lord: A Theological Aesthetics,* Erasmo Leiva-Merikakis, ed. (San Francisco: Ignatius Press, 1982).

3. The assertion that a living tradition will produce new forms through which its reality is gradually disclosed was at the heart of John Henry Newman's understanding of the development of doctrine. This is especially evident in his discussion "On the Probability of Developments in Christianity" and characterizes the third, sixth and seventh of his tests for a genuine development, namely, the power to assimilate new elements, additions that preserve the original idea and vigorous endurance because of developments. See John Henry Newman, *An Essay on the Development of Christian Doctrine* (Baltimore, Md.: Penguin Books, 1974 edition).

4. For a positive use of the term *style,* see Bernard Swain, *Liberating Leadership: Practical Styles for Pastoral Ministry* (San Francisco:

Harper and Row, 1986). Swain identifies and compares four typical styles of pastoral leadership: sovereign, parallel, semimutual and mutual.

　　5. See Tracy, "Traditions of Spiritual Practice and the Practice of Theology," 235.

2. A Ministerial Style of Theological Reflection

　　1. See James D. Whitehead and Evelyn Eaton Whitehead, *Method in Ministry: Theological Reflection and Christian Ministry* (Kansas City, Mo.: Sheed and Ward), 1995. The widespread use of the Whiteheads' book for ministerial training is somewhat ironic because it envisions theological reflection being carried out in a church setting by members of the congregation rather than in a seminary setting or training program for chaplains and lay ministers. Nonetheless, for other treatments of theological reflection in a supervisory context that refer to the Whiteheads' method, see Regina Coll, C.S.J., *Supervision of Ministry Students* (Collegeville, Minn.: Liturgical Press, 1992), 91–110; William T. Pyle and Mary Alice Seals, eds., *Experiencing Ministry Supervision: A Field-Based Approach* (Nashville, Tenn.: Broadman and Holman, 1995), 109–25; Bríd Long, "Theological Reflection in the Supervision of Pastoral Care," *The Journal of Pastoral Care* 52 (Summer 1998): 117–33. For suggestions about adapting field-education models of theological reflection to parish life, see Robert L. Kinast, "Moving Theological Reflection from Field Education to the Parish," *Chicago Studies* 31 (April 1992): 93–107, and Jean Flannelly, "Theological Reflection and Parish Ministry," *Church* 14 (Fall 1998): 29–32.

　　2. James D. and Evelyn Eaton Whitehead, *Method in Ministry*, ix.

　　3. Ibid., 3–23.

　　4. For a discussion of the Whiteheads' method as conversation, see Kathleen T. Talvacchia, "Finding God Experientially in the Tradition: Theological Reflection as Spiritual Formation," *New Theology Review* 11 (November 1998): 43–53.

　　5. Accompanying the skills of listening that the Whiteheads describe is a sense of *what* to listen for. On this point see Kinast, *Let Ministry Teach*, 48–64.

6. Using the pastoral situation as the "classroom" for theology has been a hallmark of clinical pastoral education and the foundation of the "new" pastoral theology articulated over forty years ago by Seward Hiltner in *Preface to Pastoral Theology* (Nashville, Tenn.: Abingdon Press, 1958). For a contemporary alternative to the theology-applied-to-ministry approach, see John Patton, *From Ministry to Theology: Pastoral Action and Reflection* (Nashville, Tenn.: Abingdon Press, 1990). Patton makes use of continental phenomenology to ground his style of theological reflection.

7. See Whiteheads, *Method in Ministry,* 103–42.

8. Among the features of ministerial experience that theological reflection attends to is the sense of divine mystery. On this point and for a somewhat different description of a ministerial style of theological reflection, see Anthony F. Krisak, "Theological Reflection: Unfolding the Mystery," in Robert J. Wicks, ed., *Handbook of Spirituality for Ministers* (Mahwah, N.J.: Paulist Press, 1995), 308–30.

9. To remain in touch with concrete experience, a ministerial style of theological reflection typically relies on case studies and verbatim accounts of ministerial events. For a description of how to do this, see Jeffrey H. Mahan, Barbara B. Troxell and Carol J. Allen, *Shared Wisdom: A Guide to Case Study Reflection in Ministry* (Nashville, Tenn.: Abingdon Press, 1993), 75–91. For a brief description and evaluation of the standard instruments used to describe ministerial experiences for theological reflection, see Kinast, *Let Ministry Teach,* 26–30.

10. See Whiteheads, *Method in Ministry,* 43.

11. For a different explanation of the inherent theological quality of experience based on a process-relational worldview, see Kinast, *Let Ministry Teach,* 16–23.

12. In Kinast, *Let Ministry Teach,* 68–152, the possible effects of experience on the faith tradition are described as illustration, application and interpretation. In Kinast, *Making Faith-Sense: Theological Reflection in Everyday Life* (Collegeville, Minn.: Liturgical Press, 1999), 35–75, they are described as affirmation, adaptation and conversion.

13. See Eugene C. Ulrich and William G. Thompson, "The Tradition in Theological Reflection: Scripture and the Minister," in *Method in Ministry,* 23–43.

14. For criteria to evaluate whether an action flows from reflection, see Kinast, *Let Ministry Teach,* 175–77.

3. A Spiritual Wisdom Style of Theological Reflection

1. See Thomas Groome, *Christian Religious Education: Sharing Our Story and Vision* (San Francisco: Harper and Row, 1980) and *Sharing Faith: A Comprehensive Approach to Religious Education and Pastoral Ministry* (San Francisco: HarperCollins, 1991). The approach of shared praxis described in these books has been widely implemented in catechetical curricula, including Groome's own curriculum, *Coming to Faith,* for grades K–6, published by William H. Sadlier, Inc., 9 Pine St., New York, 10005.

2. See Patricia O'Connell Killen and John de Beer, *The Art of Theological Reflection* (New York: Crossroad, 1994). This book is not to be confused with two other works bearing the same title: *The Art of Theological Reflection* by Ronald Gariboldi and Daniel Novotny (Lanham, Md.: University Press of America, 1987) and a series of 6 audiotapes entitled *The Art of Theological Reflection: Connecting Faith and Life* by John Shea (Chicago: ACTA Publications, 1997). Note also the article by Killen and de Beer, "'Everyday Theology': A Model for Religious and Theological Education," *Chicago Studies* 22 (August 1983): 191–206, and the articles by Patricia O'Connell Killen, "The Practice of Theological Reflection in Small Faith Communities," *Chicago Studies* 31 (August 1992): 189–96, and "Assisting Adults to Think Theologically," *PACE* (February 1993): 7–14. For a different approach to helping people reflect theologically on their daily experience, see Howard W. Stone and James O. Duke, *How to Think Theologically* (Minneapolis, Minn.: Fortress Press, 1996).

3. See Edward Farley, *Theologia: The Fragmentation and Unity of Theological Education* (Philadelphia: Fortress Press, 1983) and *The Fragility of Knowledge: Theological Education in the Church and the University* (Philadelphia: Fortress Press, 1988). Edward K. Braxton, utilizing the insights of Bernard Lonergan (as do Killen and de Beer), describes another version of the spiritual wisdom style of theological reflection in his book *The Wisdom Community* (Mahwah, N.J.: Paulist Press, 1980).

4. See Farley, *The Fragility of Knowledge,* 88–89.

5. See Groome, *Sharing Faith,* 8, 80–82.

6. Ibid., 30–32.

7. Ibid., 155–75.

8. Ibid., 159–60.

9. The five movements of Groome's shared Christian praxis are briefly described in *Sharing Faith* on pages 146–48 and then elaborated in chapters 6–10, pages 175–281.

10. One of the foremost proponents of using stories for theological reflection is John Shea. His most methodological account of how this may be done is found in *An Experience Named Spirit* (Chicago: The Thomas More Press, 1983), 53–88. An excellent example of his theological storytelling is *Gospel Light: Jesus Stories for Spiritual Consciousness* (New York: Crossroad, 1998).

11. See Killen and de Beer, *The Art of Theological Reflection,* viii.

12. For another discussion of the importance of feelings in theological reflection, see Kinast, *Making Faith-Sense,* 12–13.

13. For a succinct comparison between the movement toward insight and the framework for theological reflection, see Killen and de Beer, *The Art of Theological Reflection,* 74.

14. There is an obvious similarity between these four sources of experience and the Whiteheads' three sources of religiously relevant information (personal and communal experience, faith tradition and culture). Like the Whiteheads' three sources, Killen and de Beer's four sources of experience serve as a model to help people recognize when and how their experience invites theological reflection and to devise methods for reflecting in particular contexts. However, Killen and de Beer make a distinction between the positions people hold and the actions they carry out. The two are not always in harmony, although ideally they should be.

15. See Killen and de Beer, *The Art of Theological Reflection,* 61.

16. For a further discussion of the obstacles to enacting one's theological insights, see Kinast, *Making Faith-Sense,* 76–80.

4. A Feminist Style of Theological Reflection

1. One indication of the collaborative nature of feminist theology is the number of books containing essays by various authors. See for example, Ann Loades, ed., *Feminist Theology: A Reader* (Louisville, Ky.: Westminster John Knox Press, 1990); Carol P. Christ and Judith

Plaskow, eds., *Womanspirit Rising: A Feminist Reader in Religion* (San Francisco: HarperCollins, 1991); Maxine Glaz and Jeanne Stevenson Moessner, eds., *Women in Travail and Transition: A New Pastoral Care* (Minneapolis, Minn.: Fortress Press, 1991); Catherine Mowry LaCugna, ed., *Freeing Theology: The Essentials of Theology in Feminist Perspective* (San Francisco: HarperCollins, 1993); and Rebecca S. Chopp and Sheila Greeve Devaney, eds., *Horizons in Feminist Theology: Identity, Tradition, and Norms* (Minneapolis, Minn.: Fortress Press, 1997). It may also be argued that feminist theology exhibits a collective style because women function in a relational and cooperative way. Whether this is attributed to women's nature (sex) or to social conditioning (gender), it means that all else being equal, women would prefer to do theology collaboratively. From another angle, a feminist style of theological reflection is not restricted to women; it provides a model for anyone who hopes to do fruitful theological work. The encouragement of group reflection in all styles of theological reflection is an endorsement of this approach.

2. See Anne Carr, "The New Vision of Feminist Theology," in Catherine Mowry LaCugna, ed., *Freeing Theology*, 8. See also Mary Aquin O'Neill, "The Nature of Women and the Method of Theology," *Theological Studies* 56 (1995): 730–42, and for a full-length discussion of method in feminist theology, see Pamela Dickey Young, *Feminist Theology/Christian Theology: In Search of Method* (Minneapolis, Minn.: Fortress Press, 1990).

3. For a brief indication of the problems associated with using women's experience as a norm for theology, see Susan A. Ross and Elizabeth A. Johnson, "Feminist Theology: A Review of Literature," *Theological Studies* 56 (1995): 327–30. For a fuller critical assessment, see Serene Jones, "Women's Experience Between a Rock and a Hard Place: Feminist, Womanist, and *Mujerista* Theologies," in Rebecca S. Chopp and Sheila Greeve Devaney, eds., *Horizons in Feminist Theology*, 33–54.

4. Paying attention to the social location of those doing theology and interpreting normative texts has become a major element in contemporary theological method. See, for example, Fernando F. Segovia and Mary Ann Tolbert, eds., *Reading from This Place: Social Location and Biblical Interpretation in the United States*, vol. 1 (Minneapolis, Minn.: Fortress Press, 1994) and *Reading from This Place: Social Location and Biblical Interpretation in Global Perspective*, vol. 2, 1995.

5. Despite their decision not to issue a pastoral letter in response to women's concerns, the Catholic bishops in the United States clearly denounced the sinfulness of sexism in their public drafts of the letter and in the final committee report. See "One in Christ: Ad Hoc Committee Report on Women's Concerns," *Origins* (December 31, 1992): nos. 12–13. Such statements notwithstanding, the key problem remains of recognizing sexism in practice and taking the necessary steps to eradicate it.

6. For accounts of how and why women's roles were subordinated in the church, see Karen Jo Torjesen, *When Women Were Priests* (San Francisco: HarperCollins, 1995) and Rosemary Radford Ruether, *Women and Redemption: A Theological History* (Minneapolis, Minn.: Fortress Press, 1998). The most glaring example of the church's restriction of women's roles today is the continued exclusion of women from the priesthood in the Roman Catholic Church.

7. See Elisabeth Schüssler Fiorenza, *In Memory of Her: A Feminist Theological Reconstruction of Christian Origins* (New York: Crossroad, 1983) as well as her *Discipleship of Equals: A Critical, Feminist Ekklesia-logy of Liberation* (New York: Crossroad, 1993).

8. See Elizabeth A. Johnson, *She Who Is: The Mystery of God in Feminist Theological Discourse* (New York: Crossroad, 1992). For a commentary on Johnson's trinitarian theology, see Anne Hunt, *What Are They Saying About the Trinity?* (Mahwah, N.J.: Paulist Press, 1998), 22–35.

9. For an indication of the range of issues feminist theology covers, see Ann Loades, ed., *Feminist Theology: A Reader,* where biblical, historical and practical issues are discussed; Maxine Glaz and Jeanne Stevenson Moessner, eds., *Women in Travail and Transition,* where ten pastoral themes are treated; and Catherine Mowry LaCugna, ed., *Freeing Theology,* where nine theological topics are addressed.

10. See Sallie McFague, *Metaphorical Theology: Models of God in Religious Language* (Minneapolis, Minn.: Fortress Press, 1982); Mary McClintock Fulkerson, *Changing the Subject: Women's Discourses and Feminist Theology* (Minneapolis, Minn.: Fortress Press, 1994); Madonna Kolbenschlag, *Kiss Sleeping Beauty Good-Bye* (New York: Bantam Books, 1979); Megan McKenna, *Not Counting Women and Children* (Maryknoll, N.Y.: Orbis Books, 1991); Rosemary Radford Ruether, *Gaia and God: An Ecofeminist Theology*

of Earth Healing (San Francisco: HarperCollins, 1992); Elisabeth Moltmann-Wendel, *I Am My Body: A Theology of Embodiment* (New York: Crossroad, 1995); Rosemary Radford Ruether, *Women-Church: Theology and Practice of Feminist Liturgical Communities* (San Francisco: HarperCollins, 1985).

11. Feminist theologians are not alone in promoting a participative use of power. Both process and pastoral theologians have consistently taken this position. See, for example, Bernard Loomer, "Two Kinds of Power," reprinted in Bernard J. Lee, *The Future Church of 140 B.C.E.* (New York: Crossroad, 1995), 169–203, and Larry Kent Graham, "Dethroning the Demonic: Rearranging Power Through the Ministry of Care," *Care of Persons, Care of Worlds* (Nashville, Tenn.: Abingdon Press, 1992), 138–59.

12. See Rosemary Radford Ruether, *Sexism and God-Talk: Toward a Feminist Theology* (Boston: Beacon Press, 1983), 18.

13. For a discussion of this one-sided distortion of human relationships as a pastoral heresy, see Robert L. Kinast, *Process Catholicism: An Exercise in Ecclesial Imagination* (Lanham, Md.: University Press of America, 1999), 1–7.

14. See especially Rebecca S. Chopp, *The Power to Speak: Feminism, Language, God* (New York: Crossroad, 1991).

5. An Inculturation Style of Theological Reflection

1. The perspective of inculturation is just as applicable, and sometimes necessary, in traditionally Christian cultures, as Pope John Paul II's insistent appeal for a "new evangelization" in these cultures indicates. See his apostolic exhortation, *The Vocation and the Mission of the Lay Faithful in the Church and in the World* (Washington, D.C.: U.S.C.C. Publishing and Promotion Services, 1988), 95–99, and the encyclical, *The Mission of the Redeemer,* reprinted in *Origins* (January 31, 1991): 541–68. For a general discussion of inculturation, see Michael Paul Gallagher, S.J., *Clashing Symbols: An Introduction to Faith and Culture* (Mahwah, N.J.: Paulist Press, 1998). For a specific discussion of inculturation in North America, see Richard G. Cote, O.M.I., *Re-Visioning Mission: The Catholic Church and Culture in Postmodern America* (Mahwah, N.J.: Paulist Press, 1996).

2. See Robert J. Schreiter, C.PP.S., *Constructing Local Theologies* (Maryknoll, N.Y.: Orbis Books, 1985), and *The New Catholicity: Theology Between the Global and the Local* (Maryknoll, N.Y.: Orbis Books, 1997). A related work of Schreiter's, not as pertinent to the purpose of this chapter, is *Reconciliation: Mission and Ministry in a Changing Social Order* (Maryknoll, N.Y.: Orbis Books, 1992).

3. See Schreiter, *Constructing Local Theologies*, 1.

4. For a fuller discussion of contextual theologies, including five different models with examples of each, see Stephen B. Bevans, *Models of Contextual Theology* (Maryknoll, N.Y.: Orbis Books, 1992).

5. The classic expression of Black theology remains the work of James H. Cone. See his *Black Theology and Black Power* (Maryknoll, N.Y.: Orbis Books, 1997 ed.) and *God of the Oppressed* (Maryknoll, N.Y.: Orbis Books, 1997 ed.), both with new introductions. For representative works of womanist theology, see Katie Geneva Cannon, *Katie's Canon: Womanism and the Soul of the Black Community* (New York: Continuum, 1995); Emilie M. Townes, ed., *Embracing the Spirit: Womanist Perspectives on Hope, Salvation, and Transformation* (New York: Continuum, 1997). For representative works of Hispanic/Latino and *mujerista* theology, see Justo L. González, *Mañana: Christian Theology from a Hispanic Perspective* (Nashville, Tenn.: Abingdon Press, 1991); Roberto Goizueta, *Caminemos Con Jésus: Toward a Hispanic/Latino Theology of Accompaniment* (Maryknoll, N.Y.: Orbis Books, 1995); and Ada María Isasi-Díaz, *Mujerista Theology: A Theology for the Twenty-First Century* (Maryknoll, N.Y.: Orbis Books, 1996). There is also a growing voice of Asian American theologians. See, e.g., Jung Young Lee, *Marginality: The Key to Multicultural Theology* (Minneapolis, Minn.: Fortress Press, 1995) and Peter C. Phan, "Jesus the Christ with an Asian Face," *Theological Studies* 57 (1996): 399–431. There is also a *Journal of Asian and Asian American Theology*, published by the Center for Pacific and Asian American Ministries at the Claremont School of Theology in California.

6. See Schreiter, *Constructing Local Theologies*, chapter 2, 22–39, which contains the equivalent of the theological method used by the other authors reviewed in this book.

7. The pioneer in developing the theological implications of *mestizaje* is Virgilio Elizondo. See his *Mestizaje: The Dialectic of Cultural Birth and the Gospel* (San Antonio, Tex.: Mexican American Cultural

Center, 1978) and *Galilean Journey: The Mexican-American Promise* (Maryknoll, N.Y.: Orbis Books, 1983). For a discussion of Elizondo's contribution from the perspective of semiotics, see Robert Lasalle-Klein, "The Potential Contribution of C. S. Peirce to Interpretation Theory in U.S. Hispanic/Latino and Other Culturally Contextualized Theologies," *Journal of Hispanic/Latino Theology* (February 1999): 5–34. The contemporary implications of the spirituals have been articulated by James H. Cone, *The Spirituals and the Blues: An Interpretation* (Maryknoll, N.Y.: Orbis Books, 1994) and Cheryl A. Kirk-Duggan, *Exorcizing Evil: A Womanist Perspective on the Spirituals* (Maryknoll, N.Y.: Orbis Books, 1998). In these cases the benefits of a new local theology confronting a previous local theology are not confined to a particular cultural group but become a hermeneutic for interpreting the gospel for all people.

8. For another example of how semiotics contributes to theological reflection, see Raymond F. Collins, *Models of Theological Reflection* (Lanham, Md.: University Press of America, 1984). For an application of semiotics to Hispanic culture, see Alex García Rivera, *St. Martin de Porres: The "Little Stories" and the Semiotics of Culture* (Maryknoll, N.Y.: Orbis Books, 1995).

9. For the role of popular religiosity in Hispanic/Latino theology, see Orlando Espín, *The Faith of the People: Theological Reflections on Popular Catholicism* (Maryknoll, N.Y.: Orbis Books, 1997).

10. See Schreiter, *The New Catholicity,* chapter 3, 46–62.

11. Criteria for verifying the acceptability of local theologies is somewhat akin to John Henry Newman's seven tests for genuine developments of doctrine. See Newman, *An Essay on the Development of Christian Doctrine,* 122–47. There is not a comparable discussion of criteria of verification in the styles of theological reflection surveyed in the preceding chapters, although Thomas Groome does refer to three criteria in his earlier work, *Christian Religious Education,* 197–201. These criteria are consequences (of the action), continuity (with the faith tradition) and harmony with the local community of faith and larger church. The most complete discussion of, and emphasis on, criteria of validity appears in Don Browning's practical style of theological reflection, to be discussed in the next chapter.

12. For a discussion of this reciprocal, formative process, see Michael Warren, *At This Time, in This Place: The Spirit Embodied in the Local Assembly* (Harrisburg, Pa.: Trinity Press International, 1999). For

the influence of culture on the specific ministry of pastoral care, see George M. Furniss, *The Social Context of Pastoral Care* (Louisville, Ky.: Westminster John Knox Press, 1994).

6. A Practical Style of Theological Reflection

1. For helpful summaries of the reorientation of practical theology, see Don S. Browning, ed., *Practical Theology: The Emerging Field in Theology, Church, and World* (San Francisco: Harper and Row, 1983); Lewis Mudge and James Poling, eds., *Formation and Reflection* (Philadelphia: Fortress Press, 1987); and Barbara G. Wheeler and Edward Farley, eds., *Shifting Boundaries: Contextual Approaches to the Structure of Theological Education* (Louisville, Ky.: Westminster John Knox Press, 1991). For a European perspective that defines practical theology as a theological theory of action, see Gerben Heitink, *Practical Theology: History, Theory, Action Domains,* tr. Reinder Bruinsma (Grand Rapids, Mich.: Eerdmans, 1999).

2. See Don S. Browning, *A Fundamental Practical Theology: Descriptive and Strategic Proposals* (Minneapolis, Minn.: Fortress Press, 1991) and Don S. Browning, Bonnie J. Miller-McLemore, Pamela D. Couture, K. Brynolf Lyon and Robert M. Franklin, *From Culture Wars to Common Ground: Religion and the American Family Debate* (Louisville, Ky.: Westminster John Knox Press, 1997). See also Don S. Browning, David Polk and Ian S. Evison, eds., *The Education of the Practical Theologian* (Atlanta: Scholars Press, 1989).

3. See Browning, *A Fundamental Practical Theology,* 36.

4. In addition to his influence on Browning, Tracy's threefold description of theology as fundamental, systematic and practical, corresponding to the publics of the academy, church and society, helped stimulate the current redefinition of practical theology. See Tracy, *The Analogical Imagination: Christian Theology and the Culture of Pluralism* (New York: Crossroad, 1981), 47–99.

5. See Browning, *A Fundamental Practical Theology,* 47–58. For Browning, these submovements also constitute the structure for theological education, especially if supplemented by the personal history perspective characteristic of Clinical Pastoral Education (CPE). See pages 58–61.

6. See Don Browning, *Religious Ethics and Pastoral Care* (Philadelphia: Fortress Press, 1983), 53–72. James N. Poling and Donald E. Miller use the same terminology of thick descriptions as well as a similar methodology in *Foundations for a Practical Theology of Ministry* (Nashville, Tenn.: Abingdon Press, 1985), 70–82.

7. For a method of theological reflection that explicitly addresses the moral dimensions of experience using interactional theories and psychology, see Mark L. Poorman, *Interactional Morality: A Foundation for Moral Discernment in Catholic Pastoral Ministry* (Washington, D.C.: Georgetown University Press, 1993).

8. Communicating practical theology as part of public discourse and enacting its strategies in the public arena are key concerns for Dennis P. McCann and Charles R. Strain in *Polity and Praxis: A Program for American Practical Theology* (New York: Winston Press, 1985). See especially chapter 8, "An Invitation: Practical Theology as Public Discourse," 208–23.

9. See Browning, *A Fundamental Practical Theology,* chapters 9–11, 209–95.

10. For another example of uncovering theological meaning in common practices, see Dorothy C. Bass, ed., *Practicing Our Faith: A Way of Life for a Searching People* (San Francisco: Jossey-Bass Publishers, 1997).

11. See Browning, *A Fundamental Practical Theology,* 89. Browning himself has shown how this implicit theological background informs various models of psychotherapy. See *Religious Thought and the Modern Psychologies* (Philadelphia: Fortress Press, 1988).

12. For the connection between practical theology and theological ethics, see McCann and Swain, *Polity and Praxis,* chapter 6, 145–78.

13. See Browning, *A Fundamental Practical Theology,* 213–15 and *From Culture Wars to Common Ground,* chapter 10, 306–35.

7. Conclusion

1. For a critical assessment of attempts to theologize from experience, see Donald L. Gelpi, *The Turn to Experience in Contemporary Theology* (Mahwah, N.J.: Paulist Press, 1994). Gelpi finds the experiential approaches of Edward Schillebeeckx, liberation theology, process

theology and transcendental Thomism deficient and proposes a semiotic approach based on the work of Charles S. Peirce as an alternative.

2. Among the authors reviewed in this book, Thomas Groome takes the most philosophical approach to experience. The Whiteheads, Killen and de Beer, and Don Browning speak of sources, types or levels of experience. Feminist theologians and inculturation theologians take a more phenomenological approach to their respective experiences. For a philosophical discussion of experience in terms of a process-relational worldview, see Kinast, *Let Ministry Teach,* 17–22.

3. In itself, theological reflection is not a unique form of reflection. As a search for meaning, it shares a basic hermeneutical interest with other interpretive enterprises and draws upon common hermeneutical principles and techniques. This is explicitly affirmed in the work of Groome, Killen-de Beer, Schreiter and Browning. The distinctiveness of theological reflection appears in its theological interest and correlation with theological sources.

4. Theological reflection's emphasis on the meaning of discrete experiences rather than the megameaning of generic experience (universal dogma) and its assumption that every experience yields multiple meanings depending on the perspectives (social location) of the interpreters gives it a certain kinship with those same aspects of postmodernism.

Bibliography

A Ministerial Style

Buttitta, Peter K. *The Still, Small Voice That Beckons: A Theological Reflection Method for Health Ministry*. Milwaukee, Wis.: National Association of Catholic Chaplains, 1992.

Coll, Regina. *Supervision of Ministry Students*. Collegeville, Minn.: Liturgical Press, 1992.

Flannelly, Jean. "Theological Reflection and Parish Ministry." *Church* 14 (Fall 1998): 29–32.

Gross, Joe. "A Model for Theological Reflection in Clinical Pastoral Education." *The Journal of Pastoral Care* 48 (Summer 1994): 131–34.

Kemper, John C., and Eileen McMullin. *Time Apart: Reflection Models for Parish Ministers*. Villa Maria, Pa.: *The Center for Learning*, 1992.

Kinast, Robert L. *Let Ministry Teach: A Guide to Theological Reflection*. Collegeville, Minn.: Liturgical Press, 1996.

————. "Moving Theological Reflection from Field Education to the Parish." *Chicago Studies* 31 (April 1992): 93–107.

86   *What Are They Saying About Theological Reflection?*

Krisak, Anthony F. "Theological Reflection: Unfolding the Mystery," in
Robert J. Wicks, ed., *Handbook of Spirituality for Ministers*. Mahwah, N.J.: Paulist Press, 1995, 308–30.

Long, Bríd. "Theological Reflection in the Supervision of Pastoral Care."
The Journal of Pastoral Care 52 (Summer 1998): 117–33.

Mahan, Jeffrey H., Barbara B. Troxell and Carol J. Allen. *Shared Wisdom:
A Guide to Case Study Reflection in Ministry*. Nashville, Tenn.:
Abingdon Press, 1993.

Nelson, Randy A. "Doing Theology in a Clinical Setting." *The Journal of
Pastoral Care* 47 (Summer 1993): 168–79.

Patton, John. *From Ministry to Theology: Pastoral Action and Reflection*.
Nashville, Tenn.: Abingdon Press, 1990.

Pyle, William T., and Mary Alice Seals, eds. *Experiencing Ministry Supervision: A Field-Based Approach*. Nashville, Tenn.: Broadman and
Holman, 1994.

Whitehead, James D., and Evelyn Eaton Whitehead. *Method in Ministry:
Theological Reflection and Christian Ministry*. Kansas City, Mo.:
Sheed and Ward, 1995.

A Spiritual Wisdom Style

Braxton, Edward K. *The Wisdom Community*. Mahwah, N.J.: Paulist
Press, 1980.

Cobb, John B., Jr. *Becoming a Thinking Christian*. Nashville, Tenn.:
Abingdon Press, 1993.

———. *Lay Theology*. St. Louis, Mo.: Chalice Press, 1994.

Gariboldi, Ronald, and Daniel Novotny. *The Art of Theological Reflection*. Lanham, Md.: University Press of America, 1987.

Groome, Thomas. *Christian Religious Education: Sharing Our Story and
Vision*. San Francisco: Harper and Row, 1980.

————. *Sharing Faith: A Comprehensive Approach to Religious Education and Pastoral Ministry.* San Francisco: HarperCollins, 1991.

Johnson, Abigail. "Reflecting with God: Theological Reflection with Laity." *Association for Theological Field Education Journal* 1 (January 1997): 11–23.

Killen, Patricia O'Connell. "The Practice of Theological Reflection in Small Faith Communities." *Chicago Studies* 31 (August 1992): 189–96.

Killen, Patricia O'Connell and John de Beer. *The Art of Theological Reflection.* New York: Crossroad, 1994.

————."'Everyday Theology': A Model for Religious and Theological Education." *Chicago Studies* 22 (August 1983): 191–206.

Kinast, Robert L. *If Only You Recognized God's Gift: John's Gospel as a Guide to Theological Reflection.* Grand Rapids, Mich.: Eerdmans, 1993.

————. *Making Faith-Sense: Theological Reflection in Everyday Life.* Collegeville, Minn.: Liturgical Press, 1999.

Shea, John. *The Art of Theological Reflection: Connecting Faith and Life,* 6 audiotapes. Chicago: ACTA Publications, 1997.

————. *An Experience Named Spirit.* Chicago: Thomas More Press, 1983.

Stone, Howard W., and James O. Duke. *How to Think Theologically.* Minneapolis, Minn.: Fortress Press, 1996.

Talvacchia, Kathleen T. "Finding God Experientially in the Tradition: Theological Reflection as Spiritual Formation." *New Theology Review* 11 (November 1998): 43–53.

A Feminist Style

Chopp, Rebecca S. *The Power to Speak: Feminism, Language, God.* New York: Crossroad, 1991.

Chopp, Rebecca S., and Sheila Greeve Devaney, eds. *Horizons in Feminist Theology: Identity, Tradition, and Norms.* Minneapolis, Minn.: Fortress Press, 1997.

Christ, Carol P., and Judith Plaskow, eds. *Womanspirit Rising: A Feminist Reader in Religion.* San Francisco: HarperCollins, 1991.

Fulkerson, Mary McClintock. *Changing the Subject: Women's Discourses and Feminist Theology.* Minneapolis, Minn.: Fortress Press, 1994.

Glaz, Maxine, and Jeanne Stevenson Moessner, eds. *Women in Travail and Transition: A New Pastoral Care.* Minneapolis, Minn.: Fortress Press, 1991.

Johnson, Elizabeth A. *She Who Is: The Mystery of God in Feminist Theological Discourse.* New York: Crossroad, 1992.

Kirk, Pamela. "Women and God in the Church: Critique and Construction." *New Theology Review* 8 (August 1995): 19–28.

LaCugna, Catherine Mowry, ed. *Freeing Theology: The Essentials of Theology in Feminist Perspective.* San Francisco: HarperCollins, 1993.

Loades, Ann, ed. *Feminist Theology: A Reader.* Louisville, Ky.: Westminster John Knox Press, 1990.

McFague, Sallie. *Metaphorical Theology: Models of God in Religious Language.* Minneapolis, Minn.: Fortress Press, 1982.

O'Neill, Mary Aquin. "The Nature of Women and the Method of Theology." *Theological Studies* 56 (December 1995): 730–42.

Ross, Susan A., and Mary Catherine Hilkert. "Feminist Theology: A Review of Literature." *Theological Studies* 56 (1995) 327–52.

Ruether, Rosemary Radford. *Gaia and God: An Ecofeminist Theology of Earth Healing.* San Francisco: HarperCollins, 1992.

————. *Sexism and God-Talk: Toward a Feminist Theology.* Boston: Beacon Press, 1983.

————. *Women-Church: Theology and Practice of Feminist Liturgical Communities.* San Francisco: HarperCollins, 1985.

————. *Women and Redemption: A Theological History.* Minneapolis, Minn.: Fortress Press, 1998.

Schüssler Fiorenza, Elisabeth. *Discipleship of Equals: A Critical, Feminist Ekklesia-logy of Liberation.* New York: Crossroad, 1993.

————. *In Memory of Her: A Feminist Theological Reconstruction of Christian Origins.* New York: Crossroad, 1983.

Torjesen, Karen Jo. *When Women Were Priests.* San Francisco: Harper-Collins, 1995.

Young, Pamela Dickey. *Feminist Theology/Christian Theology: In Search of Method.* Minneapolis, Minn.: Fortress Press, 1990.

An Inculturation Style

Bevans, Stephen B. *Models of Contextual Theology.* Maryknoll, N.Y.: Orbis Books, 1992.

Cannon, Katie Geneva. *Katie's Canon: Womanism and the Soul of the Black Community.* New York: Continuum, 1995.

Cote, Richard G. *Re-Visioning Mission: The Catholic Church and Culture in Postmodern America.* Mahwah, N.J.: Paulist Press, 1996.

Elizondo, Virgilio. *Galilean Journey: The Mexican-American Promise.* Maryknoll, N.Y.: Orbis Books, 1983.

————. *Mestizaje: The Dialectic of Cultural Birth and the Gospel.* San Antonio, Tex.: Mexican American Cultural Center, 1978.

Gallagher, Michael Paul. *Clashing Symbols: An Introduction to Faith and Culture.* Mahwah, N.J.: Paulist Press, 1998.

Goizueta, Roberto. *Caminemos Con Jésus: Toward a Hispanic/Latino Theology of Accompaniment.* Maryknoll, N.Y.: Orbis Books, 1995.

González, Justo L. *Mañana: Christian Theology from a Hispanic Perspective.* Nashville, Tenn.: Abingdon Press, 1991.

Isasi-Díaz, Ada María. *Mujerista Theology: A Theology for the Twenty-First Century.* Maryknoll, N.Y.: Orbis Books, 1996.

Jernigan, Homer L. "Teaching Pastoral Theology from a Global Perspective." *Theological Education* 30 (Autumn 1993): 191–233.

Kemper, John C. "Doing Theological Reflection Within a Cultural Group." *East Asian Pastoral Review* 4 (1992): 427–39.

————. "Imaginative Theological Reflection." *Human Development* (Winter 1995): 17–19.

Lee, Jung Young. *Marginality: The Key to Multicultural Theology.* Minneapolis, Minn.: Fortress Press, 1995.

Pedraja, Luis G. "Doing Theology as Dialogue in the Hispanic Community." *Journal of Hispanic/Latino Theology* 5 (February 1998): 39–49.

Phan, Peter C. "Jesus the Christ with an Asian Face." *Theological Studies* 57 (September 1996): 399–431.

Schreiter, Robert J. *Constructing Local Theologies.* Maryknoll, N.Y.: Orbis Books, 1985.

————. *The New Catholicity: Theology Between the Global and the Local.* Maryknoll, N.Y.: Orbis Books, 1997.

Starkloff, Carl F. "Inculturation and Cultural Systems." *Theological Studies* 55 (March, June 1994): 66–82; 274–95.

Townes, Emilie M., ed. *Embracing the Spirit: Womanist Perspectives on Hope, Salvation, and Transformation.* New York: Continuum, 1997.

Van Beeck, Frans Jozef. "Faith and Theology in Encounter with Non-Christians." *Theological Studies* 55 (March 1994): 46–66.

Warren, Michael. *At This Time, in This Place: The Spirit Embodied in the Local Assembly.* Harrisburg, Pa: Trinity Press International, 1999.

———. "Speaking and Learning in the Local Church: A Look at the Material Conditions." *Worship* 69 (January 1995): 28–51.

A Practical Style

Arens, Edmund. *Christopraxis: A Theology of Action.* Minneapolis, Minn.: Fortress Press, 1995.

Bass, Dorothy C., ed. *Practicing Our Faith: A Way of Life for a Searching People.* San Francisco: Jossey-Bass, 1997.

Browning, Don S., *A Fundamental Practical Theology: Descriptive and Strategic Proposals.* Minneapolis, Minn.: Fortress Press, 1991.

———. *Religious Ethics and Pastoral Care.* Philadelphia: Fortress Press, 1983.

———, Bonnie J. Miller-McLemore, Pamela D. Couture, K. Brynolf Lyon and Robert M. Franklin. *From Culture Wars to Common Ground: Religion and the American Family Debate.* Louisville, Ky.: Westminster John Knox Press, 1997.

———, David Polk and Ian S. Evison, eds. *The Education of the Practical Theologian.* Atlanta: Scholars Press, 1989.

92 *What Are They Saying About Theological Reflection?*

92 *What Are They Saying About Theological Reflection?*

————. ed. *Practical Theology: The Emerging Field in Theology, Church, and World.* San Francisco: Harper and Row, 1983.

Floristán, Casiano. "Naturaleza de la Teología Práctica." *Journal of Hispanic/Latino Theology* 5 (November 1998): 5–18.

Heitink, Gerben. *Practical Theology: History, Theory, Action Domains,* tr. Reinder Bruinsma. Grand Rapids, Mich.: Eerdmans, 1999.

Kinast, Robert L. "Experiencing the Tradition Through Theological Reflection." *New Theology Review* 8 (February 1995): 6–18.

————. "Getting the Most Out of Work." *New Theology Review* 11 (August 1998): 14–22.

Lee, Bernard J. *The Future Church of 140 B.C.E.: The Hidden Revolution.* New York: Crossroad, 1995.

Lynch, Peter. "Tested by Practice," in Richard Lennan, ed., *An Introduction to Catholic Theology.* Mahwah, N.J.: Paulist Press, 1998, 164–84.

McCann, Dennis P., and Charles R. Strain. *Polity and Praxis: A Program for American Practical Theology.* New York: Winston Press, 1985.

Mudge, Lewis, and James Poling, eds. *Formation and Reflection.* Philadelphia: Fortress Press, 1987.

Poling, James N., and Donald E. Miller. *Foundations for a Practical Theology of Ministry.* Nashville, Tenn.: Abingdon Press, 1985.

Poorman, Mark L. *Interactional Morality: A Foundation for Moral Discernment in Catholic Pastoral Ministry.* Washington, D.C.: Georgetown University Press, 1993.

Smith, Thomas. *God on the Job: Finding God Who Waits at Work.* Mahwah, N.J.: Paulist Press, 1995.

Wheeler, Barbara G., and Edward Farley, eds. *Shifting Boundaries: Contextual Approaches to the Structure of Theological Education.* Louisville, Ky.: Westminster John Knox Press, 1991.

Index

Other Books in This Series

Other Books in This Series

What are they saying about the Ministerial Priesthood?
by Rev. Daniel Donovan
What are they saying about the Social Setting
of the New Testament?
by Carolyn Osiek
What are they saying about Scripture and Ethics?
(Revised and Expanded Ed.)
by William C. Spohn
What are they saying about Unbelief?
by Michael Paul Gallagher, S.J.
What are they saying about Masculine Spirituality?
by David James
What are they saying about Environmental Ethics?
by Pamela Smith
What are they saying about the Formation of Pauline Churches?
by Richard S. Ascough
What are they saying about the Trinity?
by Anne Hunt
What are they saying about the Formation of Israel?
by John J. McDermott
What are they saying about the Parables?
by David Gowler